I0149934

Jesus came to restore our eternal life with God and also positioned us to operate in complete authority and dominion in governing heaven and the earth. "KINGDOM HEIRS! DECREE THAT THANG," *provides apostolic revelation, impartation and activation, for all who desire to pray and live from an established position as a rightful heir to the throne room of God. Learn who you are and your kingly rights as a Kingdom Heir and how to pray, and abide in this Jesus authorized position so that the kingdom of God can be established in your midst.*

Kingdom Heirs! Decree That Thang!

TaquettaBaker@Kingdomshifters.com

(Website) Kingdomshifters.com

Connect with Taquetta via Facebook or YouTube

Copyright 2011 – Kingdom Shifters Ministries

Taquetta's Bio

Taquetta Baker is the founder of Kingdom Shifters
Ministries (KSM). She has authored fourteen books
and two decree CD's. Taquetta has a Master's Degree
in Community Counseling with an emphasis on
Marriage, Children and Family Counseling, a
Bachelor's Degree in Psychology and Associates Degree
in Business Administration. In addition, Taquetta has
a Therapon Belief Therapist Certification from
Therapon Institute and has 22 years of professional and
Christian Counseling experience.

Taquetta is also gifted at empowering and assisting people
with launching ministries, businesses and books and
provides mentoring, counseling and vision casting
through Kingdom Shifters Kingdom Wellness Program.
Taquetta serves on the Board of Directors for New Day
Community Ministries, Inc. of Muncie, IN. In October
2008, Taquetta graduated from the Eagles Dance
Institute under Dr. Pamela Hardy and received her
license in the area of liturgical dance. Before launching
into her own ministry, Taquetta served at her previous
church for 12 years. She was a prophet, pioneer and
leader of Shekinah Expressions Dance Ministry,
teacher, member of the presbytery board, and overseer of
the Altar Workers Ministry. Taquetta receives
mentoring and ministry covering from Bishop Jackie
Green, Founder of JGM-National PrayerLife Institute
(Phoenix, AZ), and was ordained as an Apostle on June
7, 2014.

Taquetta flows through the wells of warfare and worship
and mantles an apostolic mandate of judging and

establishing God's kingdom in people, ministries, communities, and regions. Taquetta travels in foreign missions and throughout the United States. She has mentored and established dance, altar workers, deliverance, and prophetic ministries. Taquetta ministers in the areas of fine arts, all manners of prayer, fivefold ministry, deliverance, healing, miracles, atmospheric worship, and empowers and train people in their destiny and life's vision.

Connect with Taquetta and KSM at <u>kingdomshifters.com</u> or via Facebook. For more information regarding Bishop Jackie Green at Jgmenternational.org

TABLE OF CONTENTS

Forward

There are many books on the market that show you how to declare and decree the will of God over your life. The difference between this book and many of those books is the proliferation of the word of God. You can never go wrong declaring the word of God. To speak the word over your life is the best way to establish the purpose of God in your mind, spirit and destiny. When you declare a God thing you can expect a God result. This God inspired book shows how you can boldly proclaim the word of God. The teachings and decrees are guides to help you realize the power you can step into when you stand on God's Word and vision of who you are as a kingdom heir to his throne. I encourage you to utilize this book as a tool to move you into the spiritual realm where everything is already done. The spirit realm is awaiting your authority to activate and tangibly manifest your inheritance and your destiny.

I decree blessings to all who read and apply the principles in this book!

Pastor Denise S. Millben M.Ed
Christ Temple Global Ministries

Forward

It takes a person absolutely confident in their position and relationship to the king, to boldly talk about being an heir. In fact, a son or daughter who is called an heir apparent is completely fortified as first in line to receive an inheritance. There is no legal contest to their position. That perfectly describes Taquetta as she is an heir apparent to her Father's kingdom. She is protected by divine law as she operates in all that has rightfully been appointed to her hands for kingdom work. Wealth and prosperity are securely hers. Deliverance and healing are assigned to her hands. Fivefold ministry is clearly one of the treasures passed on by her heavenly Father. Proof of good stewardship to an inheritance is the amount of proven increase that comes from the heir. Taquetta has that proof many times over in the individuals she mentors, the ministries she has impacted, and the lives that are changed because of her labor of love. She is a visionary and a pioneer. She is a demon buster and a warrior. She is an intercessor and a soldier. She is a wise counselor. Taquetta has stood strong in adversity and moved by faith in tribulation. She is in her rightful place as she now imparts to every reader the fruit of years of striving without compromise to find the place where her written declarations powerfully open the heavens and bring the glory into your situation. Read every word with expectation that the King of kings has released an heir apparent and will transform you to the place of a kingdom heir.

Blessings,

Rev. Kathy E. Williams

New Day Ministries, Muncie Indiana

DECREEING FROM HEAVENLY PLACES

As *Kingdom Heirs* it is important that we pray from an established position that Jesus restored unto us when He shed His blood, died on the cross, and resurrected with ALL power in His hands. This place re-establishes the dominion we were to have before the fall of Adam and Eve. We recognize such dominion in *Genesis 1:26-28,*

> *(Amplified)*
> *God said, Let Us [Father, Son, and Holy Spirit] make mankind in Our image, after Our likeness, and let them have complete authority over the fish of the sea, the birds of the air, the [tame] beasts, and over all of the earth, and over everything that creeps upon the earth. So God created man in His own image, in the image and likeness of God He created him; male and female He created them. And God blessed them and said to them, Be fruitful, multiply, and fill the earth, and subdue it [using all its vast resources in the service of God and man]; and have dominion over the fish of the sea, the birds of the air, and over every living creature that moves upon the earth.*

When Adam and Eve ate of the tree of good and evil, it caused a contending of dominion upon the earth between man and Satan, the serpent. This story is not the basis for this book, however, read Genesis 3 if you are not familiar with it.

Jesus came to restore our eternal life with God and also positioned us to operate once again in being able to have complete authority and dominion in governing the earth.

Ephesians 2:4-6

(KJV)
But God, who is rich in mercy, for his great love wherewith he loved us,
Even when we were dead in sins, hath quickened us together with Christ, (by grace ye are saved)
And hath raised us up together, and made us sit together in heavenly places in Christ Jesus:

(Amplified)
But God — so rich is He in His mercy! Because of and in order to satisfy the great and wonderful and intense love with which He loved us, Even when we were dead (slain) by [our own] shortcomings and trespasses, He made us alive together in fellowship and in union with Christ; [He gave us the very life of Christ Himself, the same new life with which He quickened Him, for] it is by grace (His favor and mercy which you did not deserve) that you are saved (delivered from judgment and made partakers of Christ's salvation). And He raised us up together with Him and made us sit down together [giving us joint seating with Him] in the heavenly sphere [by virtue of our being] in Christ Jesus (the Messiah, the Anointed One).

The word says that "we have been raised up in heavenly places *IN CHRIST JESUS*. *Philippians 2:9-11*, tells us that God made Jesus the name of dominion throughout the universe, and because we are now raised up with Him, our dominion has been established in Him.

Philippians 2:9-11
(KJV)
Wherefore God also hath highly exalted him, and given him a name which is above every name: That at the name of Jesus every knee should bow, of things in heaven, and things in earth, and things under the earth; And that every tongue should confess that Jesus Christ is Lord, to the glory of God the Father.

When Jesus restored our dominion, He not only gave us dominion in the earth realm, but also in heaven. He restored our right to walk with God in the cool of the day (be boldly intimate with God), and to boldly reap the fruit of heaven in the earth realm. God desires this fruitfulness and multiplication in everything we put our hands to that is of Him.

In my opinion, being seated in heavenly places means to occupy, to be positioned, to take up residence, to be established in a place or position. It isn't simply a seat of communing with Jesus, but is a place of governmental authority or rule. For example, when you come in a place and put your things down in a seat that is now your territory. Therefore, it doesn't matter if you leave that seat to mingle, use the restroom, etc., you still expect to have your seat when you return. By placing your things there, you have marked that territory and thus have established rule over that particular seat. When equating that with heaven, it's similar but your seat, position is now eternal. Because of Jesus works at the cross, you are now heir to the throne with Christ and so that's not just your seat, but your sphere. And because everything else is now under your feet, you rule with Jesus in dominion over everything that is under you....this is your position (seating). This is what it means to be established in heavenly places.

SEATED IN HEAVENLY PLACES

1. I decree I am made in the image and likeness of God, reflecting His nature, and I have complete authority over the fish of the sea, the birds/fowls of the air, the [tame] beasts, over all of the earth, and over everything that creeps upon the earth.

2. I decree that God has blessed me, and I walk in the authority of fruitfulness and supernatural multiplication. I fill the earth with God's glory and divine goodness, and as a filler, I release His heavenly kingdom into the earth.

3. I decree that I govern through a subduing anointing, using all the vast resources in the service of God and man, and rule in the likeness to which God fashioned me at creation.

4. I decree that the fall of man no longer binds or hinders my authority, for my sins are dead through the work of the cross, and I am now alive via the resurrection of Christ Jesus my glorious savior.

5. I decree that I live and govern from this heavenly place and administer the kingdom of heaven into the earthly life that I govern.

6. I fall out agreement with anything that is not from my God or from heaven and command it to loose my life and sphere of influence.

7. I decree that if it isn't in heaven, it cannot live, reside, or manifest in the earthly life that I govern.

8. I assert *Matthew 6:10* and command the kingdom of God to come now. Your kingdom is now for me! God's will be done, on earth as it is for me in heaven

9. I decree heaven is my standard for living and existing, and through the empowerment of *2Corinthians 2:5*, I cast down every other vain imagination or high thing that would exalt itself against God's knowledge and banner for my life. Be held captive unto the obedience of Christ now in Jesus name.

10. I decree that this is my set position and is non-negotiable! I belong here and have a kingly right to everything heaven has to offer.

11. I decree I am seated and rule in heavenly places with Christ Jesus.

HEIR TO THE THRONE

Galatians 4:1-7

> *(KJV)*
> *Now I say that the heir, as long as he is a child, does not differ at all from a slave, though he is master of all, but is under guardians and stewards until the time appointed by the father. Even so we, when we were children, were in bondage under the elements of the world. But when the fullness of the time had come, God sent forth His Son, born of a woman, born under the law, to redeem those who were under the law, that we might receive the adoption as sons.*
>
> *And because you are sons, God has sent forth the Spirit of His Son into your hearts, crying out, "Abba, Father!" Therefore you are no longer a slave but a son, and if a son, then an heir of God through Christ.*
>
> *Verse 7 (Amplified)*
> *Therefore, you are no longer a slave (bond servant) but a son; and if a son, then [it follows that you are] an heir by the aid of God, through Christ.*

Heir in the Greek is *Kleronomos* and means:

1. A sharer by lot.
2. Inheritor (literally or figuratively); by implication, a possessor.
3. An heir.
4. One who receives by lot.

5. In Messianic usage, one who receives his allotted possession by right of sonship.
6. One who has acquired or obtained a portion allotted to him.

Dictionary.com defines *Heir* as:

1. A person who inherits or is entitled by law or by the terms of a will to inherit the estate of another.
2. A person who succeeds or is in line to succeed to a hereditary rank, title, or office.
3. One who receives or is expected to receive a heritage, as of ideas, from a predecessor.
4. (Law) Civil law the person legally succeeding to all property of a deceased person, irrespective of whether such person died testate or intestate, and upon whom devolves as well as the rights the duties and liabilities attached to the estate
5. Any person or thing that carries on some tradition, circumstance, etc., from a forerunner.

We can discern from these definitions that a worldly heir and a heavenly heir have significant distinctions. In the world, an heir usually has to wait until the person is deceased before he or she can obtain the inheritance of that person or family lineage. However, in God's kingdom, we have already died with Jesus and rose with Him, therefore we share in the inheritance of heaven and in ruler-ship with Him. When we accept Jesus as our savior, the workings of the cross consume us and we are now adopted into the kingdom of God through grace. This grace banishes all shame, guilt and timidity of sin, and give us kingly right to approach God's throne and ask for what is needed to properly govern the earth that we have been positioned to dominate and oversee. Often we fear asking God for anything because we don't feel worthy or haven't been taught our worth. But God's word plainly lets us know that we are *Kingdom Heirs* and have favor with God through Jesus. God wants us to govern and rule victoriously and has provided all that we need so we can return to a position of dominion.

Hebrews 4:14-16

(KJV)
Seeing then that we have a great High Priest who has passed through the heavens, Jesus the Son of God, let us hold fast our confession. For we do not have a High Priest who cannot sympathize with our weaknesses, but was in all points tempted as we are, yet without sin. Let us therefore come boldly to the throne of grace, that we may obtain mercy and find grace to help in time of need.

(Message)
Now that we know what we have--Jesus, this great High Priest with ready access to God--let's not let it slip through our fingers. We don't have a priest who is out of touch with our reality. He's been through weakness and testing, experienced it all--all but the sin. So let's walk right up to

him and get what he is so ready to give. Take the
mercy, accept the help.

<u>*Boldy* in this passage of scripture is *Parresia* and means:</u>
1. frankness, bluntness, publicity; by implication, assurance, bold
2. confidence, freely, openly, plainly, boldness
3. freedom in speaking, unreservedness in speech
4. openly, frankly, i.e without concealment
5. without ambiguity or circumlocution
6. without the use of figures and comparisons
7. free and fearless confidence, cheerful courage, boldness, assurance
8. the deportment by which one becomes conspicuous or secures publicity

<u>*Throne* in that passage of scripture is *Thrao* and means:</u>
1. (to sit); a stately seat (—throne‖)
2. by implication, power or (concretely) a potentate: a throne seat
3. a chair of state having a footstool
4. assigned in the NT to kings, hence, kingly power or royalty
5. the throne of God, the governor of the world
6. to the Messiah, Christ, the partner and assistant in the divine administration
7. hence divine power belonging to Christ

8. to judges i.e. tribunal or bench, to elders

We will discuss this more in detail however, it is essential as *Kingdom Heirs* that we understand the following:

- We are royalty and have complete access to God, the governor of the entire world.
- We can boldly approach Him for assistance of our needs and for aide to properly govern the sphere of influence that He has granted us.
- We have a right to the fruit of heaven and a right to the judgment of our Father's throne.
- We have a right to judge as heirs through God's throne and to release His judgment in our midst.
- Jesus understood being tempted and the trials of the world and has provided a pathway through His workings on the cross that brought grace for us to boldly approach the throne.
- When we are governing properly through the throne of God's grace, it makes dealing with sin and trials easier. I assert this because we are in essence, approaching these matters through the kingly fruit and heart of God, rather than through our soul and fleshly nature, and thus we stand in a place of Godly character and kingly victory and dominion over them.

When we fully grasp our kingly inheritance, then we can begin to effectively rule as God intended when He first created the world. Often we perceive being before God's throne as a posture in prayer, and though this is true, as we mature in God, there should be a place where we truly see and are literally before the throne room of God. Heaven is an actual place and we have access to it via our spirit man. There are times where I see, sense and/or literally know I am standing or kneeling before the throne of God. Sometimes, such an experience can occur by faith, dreams and visions, or by literally ascending to heaven. Here are a few scriptures to encourage your faith in this area.

Psalms 24:3-4

(KJV)
Who shall ascend (go up) into the hill of the LORD? or who shall stand in his holy place? He that hath clean hands, and a pure heart; who hath not lifted up his soul unto vanity, nor sworn deceitfully.

Psalms 139:8

(KJV)
If I ascend up into heaven, thou art there: if I make my bed in hell, behold, thou art there.

Ezekiel 43:5

(KJV)
Then the Spirit lifted me up and brought me into the inner court, and the glory of the LORD filled the temple.

Isaiah 6:1-3

(KJV)

In the year of King Uzziah's death, I saw the Lord sitting on a throne, lofty and exalted, with the train of His robe filling the temple. Seraphim stood above Him, each having six wings; with two he covered his face, and with two he covered his feet, and with two he flew. And one called out to another and said, "Holy, Holy, Holy, is the LORD of hosts, The whole earth is full of His glory."

John 20:17

(KJV)

Jesus saith unto her, Touch me not; for I am not yet ascended to my Father: but go to my brethren, and say unto them, I ascend unto my Father, and your Father; and to my God, and your God.

Acts 8:39

(KJV)

When they came up out of the water, the Spirit of the Lord suddenly took Philip away, and the eunuch did not see him again, but went on his way rejoicing.

Hebrews 11:5

(KJV)

*By **faith** Enoch was translated that he should not see death; and was not found, because God had translated him: for before his translation he had this testimony, that he pleased God.*

2 Corinthians 12:1-4

(KJV)

It is not expedient for me doubtless to glory. I will come to visions and revelations of the Lord. I knew a man in Christ above fourteen years ago, (whether in the body, I cannot tell; or whether out of the body, I cannot tell: God knoweth;) such an one caught up to the third heaven. And I knew such a man, (whether in the body, or out of the body, I cannot tell: God knoweth;) How that he was caught up into paradise, and heard unspeakable words, which it is not lawful for a man to utter.

Revelations 4:1-2

(KJV)

After this I looked, and, behold, a door was opened in heaven: and the first voice which I heard was as it were of a trumpet talking with me; which said, Come up hither, and I will shew thee things which must be hereafter. And immediately I was in the spirit: and, behold, a throne was set in heaven, and one sat on the throne.

I BELONG BEFORE THE THRONE

1. By faith I ascend before Your throne of grace.

2. I decree I am literally positioned before Your throne God, honoring who You are in and to me and submitting and surrendering who I am in and through You.

3. I decree I am no longer a slave, a bond servant, but am postured in sonship with God through the works of Christ Jesus.

4. I decree I am blessed here. I decree there is peace and rest here. I decree I am empowered here. I am worthy as You welcome me to approach You and abide with You; I bow as a covenant *Heir*, yielding worship and praise before Your throne of mercy and grace.

5. You have done great works for me through the judgment and justice of Your throne and I bless You for Your works Oh Lord on my behalf. I decree that residing here with You is my rightful place as a *Kingdom Heir* to Your throne. I am joint *heir* with You Jesus. You are my Lord...my King, the crowned prince...my greatest inheritance....the successor of all.

6. I decree that I govern through Your throne, entrenched in a subduing anointing, using all the vast resources in the service of God and man, and rule in the likeness to which You fashioned me at creation. Even now I loose the wind of the Holy Ghost and a subduing anointing to release Your likeness into all that

requires activation, creation and recreation in my midst.

7. I decree that the fall of man no longer binds or hinders my authority, for my sins are dead through the work of the cross, and I am now alive via the resurrection of Christ Jesus, my glorious savior. I arise in resurrection power and decree the life and light of Christ and the throne of grace over all that concerns me in Jesus name.

8. I decree that I live and govern from this heavenly place and administer the kingdom of heaven to produce life and that more abundantly, restoration and kingly establishment into my earthly life now in the name of Jesus.

9. I fall out of agreement with anything that is not from God or from heaven and command it to loose my life and sphere of influence effective immediately in the name of Jesus.

10. I decree if it is not in heaven, it cannot live, reside, or manifest in my earthly life (say three times).

11. I assert *Matthew 6:10* and command the kingdom of God to come now. Your kingdom is now for me! God's will be done now, on earth as it is for me in heaven. Heaven infuse my earth now. Let the very existence of heaven become the very nature of my earthly sphere now in the name Jesus.

12. I decree Your grace and unconditional love restored me as an *Heir* in Your kingdom and

granted me this kingly position. There is so much love before You. I receive and bask in the deliverance and healing of Your outstretched love. Through Your love and grace, I take my rightful place and profess dominion now in the name of Jesus.

13. As a *Kingdom Heir*, I do not squander my inheritance. I govern appropriately and in a healthy manner. The throne of love has made me healthy and as I assert dominion within the earth, I mature in love.

14. I decree that my decisions are in alignment with Your will Lord and the calling and destiny You have placed on my life and sphere of influence.

15. Even now I stand boldly asking and receiving wisdom, guidance, revelation, and understanding regarding who I am, what I am called to do, and the direction and tools necessary to birth forth my calling and destiny in fullness.

16. You have predestined me, called me, justified me and empowered me with Your miraculous glory (Romans 8:30).

17. With such a pre-orchestrated release to journey toward a successful and purposeful end, You are not withholding any good thing from me. I decree *Psalms 84:11* over my life, lineage, and sphere of influence, and contend that "*the LORD God is my sun and shield: the LORD will give me grace and glory: no good thing will He withhold from me because I walk uprightly.*"

18. I further declare the Amplified version and proclaim, "*the Lord God is my sun and shield; the Lord bestows [present] grace and favor and [future] glory (honor, splendor, and heavenly bliss)! No good thing will He withhold from me, His royal seed, as I strive daily to walk uprightly.*"

19. I am a *Kingdom Heir* to the Only God in the entire universe! My Lord is King Jesus! Through Your authority, I willingly and boldly release Your will for me and all that concerns me into my sphere of influence. I administer the pleasures of Your heaven and the judgments of Your kingdom. Your kingly fruit overtakes me and all that I entail; for I Your *Kingdom Heir*, belong before and judge through Your throne!

PRAISE RELEASED FROM HIS HEAVENLY COURTS

There are instances during prayer or praise and worship, whether in my home or church, that I will thunderously yell the name of "*Jesus*" and literally feel myself ascending into the heavens. I also know during this time that a judgment is being released, as I can feel and even see at times, the atmosphere around me shift and the fruit of God being released in and among the people, into my sphere of influence, or into whatever situation I am contending for. Sometimes, the Holy Spirit will lead me to bellow out the name of *Jesus* to the North, South, East and West and as well declare His name under me and into the heavenlies. Depending on the circumstances, there are instances I can sense warfare and demonic oppression fleeing and the presence of God's refuge swirling around me. One day when listening to a sermon on the courts of heaven, the minister quoted *Psalms 100:4-5* and immediately the Holy Spirit let me know that this is what I had been experiencing when I yelled the name "*Jesus*." I therefore, begin to study and seek God further regarding a revelation of this passage of scripture.

Psalms 100:4-5
> *(KJV)*
> *Enter into his gates with thanksgiving, and into his courts (a place of law & judicial rule) with praise: be thankful unto him, and bless his name.*

*For the LORD is good; his mercy is everlasting;
and his truth endureth to all generations.*

<u>*Praise* in this scripture is *Tehilla* and is defined as:</u>
1. praise, song or hymn of praise
2. praise, adoration, thanksgiving (paid to God)
3. act of general or public praise
4. praise-song (as title)
5. praise (demanded by qualities or deeds or attributes of God)
6. of Damascus, of God
7. renown, fame, glory, the object of praise, possessor of renown

<u>The primitive root word of *Tehilla* is *Hahal* which is defined as:</u>
1. to shine, to shine (fig. of God's favor), to flash forth light
2. to praise, boast, be boastful
    a) (Qal)
       - to be boastful
       - boastful ones, boasters (participle)
    b) (Piel)
       - to praise
       - to boast, make a boast
    c) (Pual)

- to be praised, be made praiseworthy, be commended, be worthy of praise
d) (Hithpael) to boast, glory, make one's boast
e) (Poel) to make a fool of, make into a fool
f) (Hithpoel) to act madly, act like a madman

This isn't a quiet praise. It isn't mumbled under ones' breath, spoken with timidity or in a nonchalant manner. This praise is one that yields abandoned adoration to the Lord. It is a bellow that boasts of His fame and glory. It is a praise that declares that He is Lord and judge of all, while relinquishing a total surrendering of self while decreeing it. We are to enter into His gates thanking Him for what He has done and into His courts with loud maddening praises.

The Message Bible version of Psalms 100:4-5 states:

> *Enter with the password: "Thank you!" Make yourselves at home, talking praise. Thank him. Worship him. For GOD is sheer beauty, all-generous in love, loyal always and ever.*

Dictionary.com defines *Password* as:
1. a secret word or expression used by authorized persons to prove their right to access, information, etc., a secret word given for entry

2. a word or other string of characters, sometimes kept secret or confidential, that must be supplied by a user in order to gain full or partial access to a multiuser computer system or its data resources.

Synonyms for the word password are as followed:

countersign	ticket
open	watchword word
sesame	
identification	
parole key	
phrase	
key word	
signal	

Even though *Jesus* is indeed the name above every name, it is simply one of the many passwords the Lord has given me and that I recognize releases His power and judgment. I do highly recommend its usage, however, God can give you any word phrase, song, etc., so seek Him for what that is. I am simply sharing my experience to bring greater revelation and understanding to releasing God's judgment through the heavenly courts as I have witnessed it.

In the natural realm, when we go to court, it is for the purpose of conducting serious business. We aren't going there to hangout, watch a movie, chat with our friends, etc. Generally when we attend a court proceeding, it is because we have been summoned, we have initiated a judgment, we are being prosecuted, or to settle a matter that require a court ruling.

Dictionary.com defines *Court* as:

1. a place where justice is administered
2. a judicial tribunal duly constituted for the hearing and determination of cases
3. a session of a judicial assembly
4. an area open to the sky and mostly or entirely surrounded by buildings, walls, etc.
5. a high interior usually having a glass roof and surrounded by several stories of galleries or the like
6. a stately dwelling
7. a short street
8. a smooth, level quadrangle on which to play tennis, basketball, etc.
9. one of the divisions of such an area
10. the residence of a sovereign or other high dignitary; palace
11. a sovereign's or dignitary's retinue

Though the heavenly courts are administered a tad bit different, the process for which the court proceedings occur is the same. The main differences in a heavenly court are as followed:

- The Judge, God almighty is on our side.

> **Psalms 75:7** - *But God is the judge: he puts down one, and sets up another.*

- Jesus is our advocate, our lawyer, and has already been mediating for us.

> **1Timothy 2:5** - *For there is one God, and one mediator between God and men, the man Christ Jesus; (KJV)*
>
> **1John 2:1-2** - *My dear children, I am writing this to you so that you will not sin. But if anyone does sin, we have an advocate who pleads our case before the Father. He is Jesus Christ, the one who is truly righteous. 2 He himself is the sacrifice that atones for our sins — and not only our sins but the sins of all the world. (NLT)*

- The cloud of witnesses can relate and testify to the challenges and rewards of our journey in the Lord.

> **Hebrews 12:1-2** - *Wherefore seeing we also are compassed about with so great a cloud of witnesses, let us lay aside every weight, and the sin which doth so easily beset us, and let us run with patience the race that is set before us, Looking unto Jesus the author and finisher of our faith; who for the joy that was set before him endured the cross, despising the shame, and is set down at the right hand of the throne of God.*

- The court is set up to bring us victory that Jesus already conquered for us by dying on the cross and resurrecting with all power in His hands.

> **Romans 8:1-5** - *There is therefore now no condemnation to those who are in Christ Jesus, who do not walk according to the flesh, but according to the Spirit. For the law of the Spirit of life in Christ Jesus has made me free from the law of sin and death. For what the law could not do in that it was weak through the flesh, God did by sending*
> *His own Son in the likeness of sinful flesh, on account of sin: He*
> *condemned sin in the flesh, that the righteous requirement of the law might be fulfilled in us who do not walk according to the flesh but according to the Spirit. For those who live according to the flesh set their minds on the things of the flesh, but those who live according to the Spirit, the things of the Spirit.*

Several years ago I had several tumors in my reproductive area and after much contending for healing and going back and forth to the doctors, I was told everything related to my reproductive system was dead, it was very possible I had cancer, and that my only option was to have a hysterectomy. The Lord had promised me that I would be married and have children so I was quite challenged by the diagnosis. I remained steadfast in the promises of the Lord in that some kind of way, whether He would give me new organs, etc., I would indeed one day be married and have children.

Friday after I was told surgery was necessary, while praying the Holy Spirit led me into a vision, where I was sitting in a courtroom in a black suit. I was very relaxed to the point of being reclined in my seat. The prosecutors however, were really being hostile towards me. They accused me of believing God for a miracle, believing God would heal me, and believing that God was going to bring victory to my situation. Everything they said about me was indeed true as I had stood so fervently on the promise God had spoken, that for months, I literally quoted four pages of healing scriptures every four hours. The prosecutors shouted how guilty I was and it echoed throughout the courtroom. Then I heard the Lord say the word *"acquittal." "You will be acquitted of this situation."* As I arose from the vision, an overwhelming peace came over me and I logged on the internet to conduct an in-depth study of what it meant to be acquitted.

Answers.com defines *Acquittal* as:

1. judgment, as by a jury or judge, that a defendant is not guilty of a crime as charged
2. the state of being found or proved not guilty
3. An acquittal is not a finding of innocence; it is simply a conclusion that the prosecution has not proved its case beyond a reasonable doubt. Acquit pronounce not guilty of criminal

Thesaurus: A freeing or clearing from accusation or guilt: exculpation, exoneration, vindication. See law

One great factor I learned about being acquitted is that once you have been found not guilty in a court of law you cannot be tried again for the same crime. This is called double jeopardy.

Definition of *Double Jeopardy* from Nolo's Plain English Law Dictionary:

> *A rule from the Fifth Amendment to the U S Constitution that prohibits a criminal defendant from being twice made to stand trial for the same offense. A defendant is put "in jeopardy" once the jury is sworn. If the prosecutor moves to dismiss the case after that, the defendant cannot be retried. When a judge dismisses a case, however, a retrial is generally possible unless the dismissal was engineered by the prosecutor's misconduct, or there was no overriding necessity to dismiss the case. Double jeopardy protects defendants only for retrials brought within the original jurisdiction, which is why a defendant can be tried in federal court after being tried in state court. Double jeopardy does not prevent trial in a civil court on underlying facts that previously formed the basis of a criminal trial.*

In God's court of law He has His own standards for those who are in Him. A few of them are as followed:

Nahum 1:9
> *(NIV)*

*Whatever they plot against the LORD he will
bring to an end; trouble will not come a second
time.*

(KJV)
*What do you imagine against the LORD? he will
make an utter end:*
affliction shall not rise up the second time.

Romans 5:16

(God's Word)
*There is also no comparison between [God's] gift
and the one who sinned. The verdict which
followed one person's failure condemned
everyone. But, even after many failures, the gift
brought God's approval.*

Romans 8:1

(Message)
*With the arrival of Jesus, the Messiah, that
fateful dilemma is resolved. Those who enter into
Christ's being-here-for-us no longer have to live
under a continuous, low-lying black cloud.*

(KJV)
*There is therefore now no condemnation
(damnatory sentence) to them which are in
Christ Jesus, who walk not after the flesh, but
after the Spirit.*

In my vision, I was indeed guilty of the statements
the prosecutors where accusing me of. But what
God was acquitting me of was the sickness that the
enemy had released upon my womb. To make a

long story short, I did have surgery but when the doctors opened me up, there was no sign of cancer and all my reproductive organs were alive and working properly. The tumors and cysts were lying on top of my organs or were loosely twisted around them, so all the doctors had to do was remove the devil's mess. The Lord also declared such an acquittal that the hospital wrote off all my bills and many of my doctors decreased a percentage of my bills or wrote them off as well.

Though this was a vision, there are times when I will simply ascend into the heavens during prayer and by faith enter the courtroom. There are instances where I see the actual courtroom and there are instances I just know I am there. I also have experiences where I am simply ascended in the heavenlies and the Lord will lead me to decree out judgment against my adversaries or administer divine judgment into the situations I am praying for. Unlike in my dream, there are situations that I pray for where sin is involved and the enemy has a legal right to harass me or those I am praying for. To counterattack this, I begin most of my prayers by applying the cleansing blood of Jesus to any sins I have committed, my family sins, the sins of my church, friends, and in some instances I even repent on behalf of my community and nation.

Matthew 5:25-26 encourages us to:

> *(KJV)*
> *Agree with thine adversary quickly, whiles thou art in the way with him; lest at any time the adversary deliver thee to the judge, and the judge*

deliver thee to the officer, and thou be cast into prison. Verily I say unto thee, Thou shalt by no means come out thence, till thou hast paid the uttermost farthing.

(NIV)
Settle matters quickly with your adversary who is taking you to court. Do it while you are still with him on the way, or he may hand you over to the judge, and the judge may hand you over to the officer, and you may be thrown into prison.

Once I agree with my adversary and acknowledge that I have sinned, God can forgive me and release the judgment of grace that Jesus brought into my life when He shed His blood to atone me for my sins and curses. I can then place my petitions before the court and ask God to decree out His judgment or through the leading of the Holy Spirit decree out His judgment in the areas I am praying for.

I have heard and studied many ways in which one can petition the heavenly courts and I have participated in a few. For example, one can write their petitions down (those areas they desire healing, deliverance, God's will released, etc.) and then by faith enter the courts of God, call for a hearing, share their petitions and ask God to release judgment. This one is very beneficial if this is your first time pursuing the courts of heaven. It is practical and can be done in faith that God hears you and will release judgment on your behalf.

As I stated earlier, there are instances when I will just yell *Jesus* during prayer and/or praise and worship, and will immediately enter the courts. Often during praise and worship, I can sense when our praise has shifted from not just exalting and thanking the Lord but releasing judgment.

During this time, one can sense an authority rise in the people and the atmosphere and it's as if the praise is damaging the demonic kingdom.

Psalms 149:5-9 declares:

> *(KJV)*
> *Let the high praises of God be in their mouth, and a twoedged sword in their hand; To execute vengeance upon the heathen, and punishments upon the people; To bind their kings with chains, and their nobles with fetters of iron; To execute upon them the judgment written: this honour have all his saints. Praise ye the LORD.*

Judgment in this scripture is *Misphat* and means:

1. a verdict (favorable or unfavorable) pronounced judicially, especially a sentence or formal decree (human or (participant's) divine law, individual or collective), including the act, the place, the suit, the crime, and the penalty; abstractly, justice, including a participant's right or privilege (statutory or customary), or even a style: adversary, ceremony, charge, crime, custom, desert, determination, discretion, disposing, due, fashion, form, to be judged

2. judgment, justice, ordinance

3. act of deciding a case

4. place, court, seat of judgment
5. process, procedure, litigation (before judges)
6. case, cause (presented for judgment)
7. sentence, decision (of judgment)
8. execution (of judgment)
9. time (of judgment)

It is important that we come into greater revelation of how our praise impacts God and thus impacts the powers of darkness. There are times when our praise is more than just comments of appreciation, and through praise we can ascend without even realizing it and activate the vengeance of God against the whiles of the enemy. I have witnessed great deliverance and total shifts in regions when high praises bellow from the heirs of God. I urgently encourage you to seek the Lord on further revelation of the heavenly courts and ask Him to reveal ways to you can execute His judgment in your midst.

DECREEING HEAVENLY JUDGMENT

1. Lord I recognize as a *Kingdom Heir* that thanking You gets me through the gates but exaltation gives me access to Your courts. I therefore, willingly, enter Your gates with thanksgiving; I enter Your courts with praise.

2. I declare Your name in a vicious bellow, *JESUSSSSSSSSSSSS*, into all the universe. I decree a clearing of every force that would oppose me, asserting my rightful place in the heavens and the earth realm.

3. To the North, South, East and West, I declare *JESUSSSSSSS*! Beneath me and to the heavens above I declare *JESUSSSSSSS*!

4. I boast of Your fame and rally a standing ovation among the heavens that ignites Your presence to execute vengeance and punishments on my behalf and all that concerns me; to bind demonic kings and pesky nobles with fetters of iron. I COME LORD JESUS! I COME BEFORE
YOU LORD GOD, THE MOST POWERFUL KING IN ALL THE
UNIVERSE! As I enmesh with Your kingdom, I execute upon all that opposes me, the judgment written in Your word.

5. For Your word says:

- ➤ In all things, I overwhelmingly conquer through Your love (Romans 8:37).
- ➤ No weapon formed against me will succeed. I will silence every voice raised against me as these are the benefits and vindications of Your servants (Isaiah 54;17).
- ➤ I have overcome the world for greater are You in me than He that is in the world (1John 4:4).
- ➤ I have safe passages to walk on snakes and scorpions for You have given me protection and authority against every assault and power of the enemy (Luke 10:19).
- ➤ Many evils confront the consistently righteous, but You Lord deliver me out of them all (Psalms 34:19).

6. I thank You Lord for Your word that does not return void unto You; and even now I declare I am standing in Your heavenly courts, consumed by Your swirling promises.

7. I am open to being judged by You Father. I command my eyes to be enlightened to see Your courts, my ears to hear Your judgments, my senses to be in tune to Your movement and the vibration of Your heart and workings.

8. I trust Your judgments, counsel, verdict and thank You that You are for me and have established Your courts to rein victory in my favor.

9. I repent for any personal sin, family and generational sin, sins of my church, community

and nation; and loose the blood of Jesus to cleanse my very existence of the stench of sin and soul wounds, and every demonic legality or unlawful harassment of the enemy (spend time cleansing sin and wounded areas as the Holy Spirit leads).

10. I decree Your name Jesus over every sin, over every wound. I decree victory through Your name over every demonic force that would oppress, infect and affect me and all that concerns me.

11. I lay my petitions upon the mercy seat of the courts and as a *Kingdom Heir*, I exchange them for grace and mercy and the full workings of Jesus Christ being the savior and advocate of my life and destiny. (Write and/or speak out your petitions before God and surrender them to His will in exchange for grace and mercy and the works of Jesus).

> - I petition all sickness and affliction for healing and wholeness.
> - I exchange poverty and lack for the wealth and prosperity of Your kingdom and a generosity that never runs dry.
> - I put on garments of praise as I cast off heaviness.
> - I am empowered by joy and strength as I receive Your surpassing peace and will for my life.

➤ I decree the sunrise is breaking through the darkness of life's challenges as emptiness dismantles the blunders of the enemy.

12. In asserting my authority, I thank You for forgiveness and even as I forgive others, I declare my deliverance and stand as a yielded vessel willing to be used to further release judgment in my midst.

13. Even now, I stand in Your word and decree Your judgment that: ➤ I have received the blessings of Abraham and the infilling of the Holy Spirit by the works of Jesus Christ and declare redemption personally and generationally from every curse of the Law (Galatians 3:13-14).

> ➤ Deliverance, healing, and liberty is my claimed portion because You Christ Jesus, were wounded for my transgressions, You were bruised for my iniquities: the chastisement of my peace was upon You; and with Your stripes I am healed (Isaiah 53:5).
>
> ➤ I decree victory over death, destruction, tragedy, theft, and murder, for these are the works of the enemy who You have overcome.
>
> ➤ I decree and administer life and that more abundantly in every area of my existence and sphere of influence. Death be overcome, God's judgment of life has consumed You.

Resurrection life prevail now in every facet of my life in the name of Jesus (John 10:10).

➤ As Lord of the universe, Your verdict can't be overturned, annulled, abolished, or voided. It is perfecting, performing, accomplishing, initializing and executing all that You ordained for my life and destiny (Isaiah 55:11)

➤ I thank You and speak forth Your judgment of atonement, redemption, acquittal and exoneration of all charges of the enemy. I therefore, command every effect of all demonic charges to be expelled from my life in Jesus name (Isaiah 8:10)

14. I thank You Lord for executing Your judgment written for me and all that concerns me. I praise You for the fullness of Your will being exceedingly accomplished on my behalf. It's a finished work of Your heavenly judgment (Ephesians 3:20).

HEAVENLY KEY HOLDERS

Matthew 16:19

(KJV)
And I will give unto thee the keys of the kingdom of heaven: and whatsoever thou shalt bind on earth shall be bound in heaven: and whatsoever thou shalt loose on earth shall be loosed in heaven.

(Amplified)
I will give you the keys of the kingdom of heaven; and whatever you bind (declare to be improper and unlawful) on earth must be what is already bound in heaven; and whatever you loose (declare lawful) on earth must be what is already loosed in heaven.

Bind is Deo in the Greek and means:

1.   To bind (in various applications, literally or figuratively):
2.   be in bonds, knit, tie, wind, fasten 3. fasten with chains, to throw into chains
4. metaph.

> A. Satan is said to bind a woman bent together by means of a demon, as his messenger, taking possession of the woman and preventing her from standing upright
>
> B. to bind, put under obligation, of the law, duty etc.
>   • to be bound to one, a wife, a husband

- to forbid, prohibit, declare to be illicit

Heavens in the *Greek* is *Ouranos* and means:

1. the sky; by extension, heaven (as the abode of God); by implication, happiness, power, eternity; specially, the Gospel (Christianity)
2. the vaulted expanse of the sky with all things visible in it

    A. the universe, the world

    B. the aerial heavens or sky, the region where the clouds and the tempests gather, and where thunder and lightning are produced

    C. the sidereal or starry heavens

    - the region above the sidereal heavens, the seat of order of things eternal and consummately perfect where God dwells and other heavenly beings

Having keys denotes authority in whatever jurisdiction to which a person has been given access. The word says that God desires to give us the keys to the kingdom of heaven. Having the keys of heaven is indicative of our royal power, kingship, dominion, and rule. This rule is not just within heaven but within the earth realm, and thus gives the power and authority to assert God's law according to what's already done in heaven. But first it is essential to have revelation to what's occurring in heaven. We can acquire such information from God's word, yet this also requires us to begin accessing heaven, communing with God about heaven, and having a mindset of living from our heavenly realm, so we can know what judgments are lawful to release within the earth.

Psalms 1:1-3 reveals,

(KJV)

Blessed is the man who walks not in the counsel of the ungodly, nor stands in the path of sinners, nor sits in the seat of the scornful; But his delight is in the law of the Lord, and in His law he meditates day and night. He shall be like a tree planted by the rivers of water, that brings forth its fruit in its season, whose leaf also shall not wither; and whatever he does shall prosper.

(Amplified)

Blessed, (happy, fortunate, prosperous, and enviable) is the man who walks and lives not in the counsel of the ungodly [following their advice, their plans and purposes], nor stands [submissive and inactive] in the path where sinners walk, nor sits down [to relax and rest] where the scornful [and the mockers] gather. But his delight and desire are in the law of the Lord, and on His law (the precepts, the instructions, the teachings of God) he habitually meditates (ponders and studies) by day and by night. And he shall be like a tree firmly planted [and tended] by the streams of water, ready to bring forth its fruit in its season; its leaf also shall not fade or wither; and everything he does shall prosper [and come to maturity].

Kingdom Keys are essential because they release the strategies necessary to be specifically aligned with the Lord, while providing wisdom regarding how to discern and operate in each season, such that we continually prosper no matter what is occurring in our life or the world around us.

The word *Meditate* in the Hebrew is *Haga* and means:

1. to murmur (in pleasure or anger);
2. to ponder, imagine, meditate, mourn, mutter, muse
3. roar, sore, speak, study, talk, utter, growl, devise

I just love this definition because in the English language, mediate is considered a quiet pondering or something done within one's self. But this Hebrew definition lets us know that meditation is a stance, a position taken in the law of the Lord. And though at times it can be tranquil, it can also be a boisterous roaring, growling, decisive, reflection regarding the statutes of the Lord *(Matthew 11:12 - And from the days of John the Baptist until now the kingdom of heaven suffereth violence, and the violent take it by force)*. This meditative position doesn't walk in the counsel of the ungodly, it doesn't stand in the pathway of sinners, and it doesn't sit amongst the scornful. It's an exalted position, willingly and purposefully wrapped in the law of the Lord. There is such a rooting and solidified foundation in this place where a person never leaves it. Delighting in God becomes a lifestyle. His laws govern our every move and His fruit continually radiates from our lives.

Binding and loosing is a judgment that releases the statutes of God within our sphere. It is God's desire to give us the keys to be able to release these judgments with complete accuracy that causes the earthly world we govern to resemble and manifest the heavenly kingdom that we rule. An honorable king doesn't want to simply become richer while everyone and everything else around him suffers and only becomes poorer. An honorable king desires those around him, that which he governs, to reflect (meditate) the wealth and goodness of who he is, what he possess, and walks in. This is what God desires for us. He desires us to truly manifest our heavenly inheritance within our earthly sphere of influence. This requires us to delight and embrace our heavenly kingdom, so that God can release the keys necessary to assert judgment that brings heaven in our midst.

AUTHORITATIVE KEYS

1. I decree that I do not walk in the counsel of the ungodly, nor stand in the path of sinners, nor sit in the seat of the scornful. I posture myself in delight before You Oh God, meditating on Your statutes continually, contending for Your laws to become my lifestyle (Psalms 1).

2. I come in the volume of the book that is written of me and decree that because I delight to do Your will, Your laws are constantly written in my heart (Psalms 40:7-8).

3. I decree that in this eternal position, I seek to strategically possess the keys to the kingdom of heaven and it is God's delight to release these keys to me.

4. Because I have mediated on the Lord, I possess full understanding of the usage of the keys to which I have jurisdiction. And whatsoever I bind on earth is already bound in heaven. Whatsoever I loose on earth is already loosed in heaven (Matthew 16:19).

5. I declare to be illicit everything which is not a part of my heavenly home, and declare the laws of heaven are now in full operation in the laws of the land to which I own and govern.

6. Just like the Lord threw Satan and His followers out of heaven, I decree that my jurisdiction is now an extension of heaven. I release the angels who are to work with me and my power base, to go forth and bind up principalities and powers, ruling spirits, and spiritual wickedness

in high places. Dispel where necessary, until God and His kingdom becomes the ultimate stronghold in my sphere of influence (Psalms 91:11).

7. I decree as a *Kingdom Heir*, I possess relentless keys. Keys that ➤ locks and unlocks doors, gateways, strongholds, realms

   ➤ administers answers, wise counseling, understanding, and supernatural revelation and fear of the Lord

   ➤ delivers cures, healthiness, breakthrough, encouragement, supernatural strength and empowerment, hope, and unwavering faith

   ➤ release the attributes, character, image, fruit and produce of God and His kingdom

   ➤ salvation, a yearning for more, maturity and continual kingly growth

   ➤ shifts people, environments, atmospheres, climates, regions

   ➤ establish God's laws and affect the political agenda and protocol of communities, cities, nations, and the universe

   ➤ build up and produce continual growth in myself, all that concerns me, in those I am to impact, and in all that I encounter.

8. For I am like a tree planted by the rivers of water. I decree I bring forth fruit in each

season. Because I am a heavenly key holder and delight in the statutes of God, there is not a season I do not produce. My leaf and lineage never withers. It continuously prospers from now till eternity.

RELEASING THE KINGDOM

1. I decree that the kingdom of God in my life and sphere of influence is not a matter of eating and drinking, but is a full spiritual and natural inheritance that is cultivated, displayed and experienced in the fullness of righteousness, peace and joy in the Holy Spirit (Romans 14:7).

2. For I seek first Your kingdom God and Your righteousness, and because my mind is stayed on You, all these things are added unto me (Matthew 6:33).

3. All the ends of the world shall remember and turn unto You Oh Lord: and all the kindreds of the nations worship before You. For the kingdom is Yours Lord's and You are Governor among the nations. All dust bow and worshipped as none are kept alive without You. None can claim righteousness without You (Psalms 22:27-28).

4. I decree that all my works shall praise and immeasurably bless You; that my life pursues avenues to gloat of Your power, to make known Your mighty acts...spew forth the glorious majesty of Your kingdom (Psalms 145:10-12).

5. For Your Kingdom Lord is an everlasting kingdom, and Your dominion endures throughout all generations. You mount up all that fall, and raise all those that are bowed down.

6. I decisively decree that in my sphere, the eyes of all wait upon thee; and You provide meat in due season. You open Your hand as Jehovah Jireh, and satisfy the desire of every living thing (Psalms 145:13-21).

7. Therefore, we are blessed even when we appear poor in spirit...feel hopeless, lost, discontent; for thine is the kingdom of heaven (Matthew 5:3).

8. We are blessed when persecuted for righteousness' sake: for thine is the kingdom of heaven (Matthew 5:10).

9. Me and my sphere of influence, do not fear or fret, because as a *Kingdom Heir*, I believe wholeheartedly that it is Your good pleasure Father to give us the kingdom (Luke 12:32).

10. For unto us is given to know the mysteries of Your Kingdom (Luke 8:10).

11. When my family and I are in need, I decree out the kingdom. When a shift needs to manifest in my life and all that concerns me, I decree out Your Kingdom. I declare that my riches are supplied through the Kingdom (Philippians 4:19).

12. Even now I pray as You taught the disciples to pray: *My Father which art in heaven, Hallowed be thy name. Thy kingdom come. Thy will be done in earth, as it is in heaven. Give me this day my daily bread. And forgive me of my debts, as I forgive my debtors. And lead me not into temptation, but deliver me from evil: For thine is the kingdom, and*

the power, and the glory, forever. Amen (Matthew 6:9-15 9),

13. I bless You Jesus for Your example of prayer and example of journeying throughout all the cities and villages, teaching in their synagogues, and preaching the gospel of the kingdom, while healing every sickness and every disease among the people. I take my position as Kingdom Heir and go about preaching the gospel of the kingdom and healing every sickness and every disease among the people (Matthew 9:35).

14. I do as You did Jesus, speaking forth the kingdom of God unto all; healing all that need healing (Luke 9:11).

15. I preach declaring that the kingdom of heaven is at hand (Matthew 10:7, Luke 8:1).

16. I do not coward to violence for as a *Kingdom Heir*, I the violent, forcibly take back the world and all the enemy Has stolen from Your Kingdom (Matthew 11:12).

17. For even as You have provided me with the *Kingdom Keys*, I bind and loose demonic forces and powers and all manners of evils, while releasing and establishing Your kingdom, Your judgment, Your rule, in every place (Matthew 15:19).

18. I decree the Kingdom of God is at hand and is manifesting in my body, mind, spirit, soul, character, personality, emotions, will, appetite, giftings, ministry, sphere of influence and has invaded all those that concerns me (Matt 3-2).

19. As Your Kingdom invades, I release Your healing, Your deliverance, Your joy, Your righteousness, Your Holiness, Your goodness, Your power, Your peace (Luke 9:2, Luke 10:9).

20. Great and majestic are Your miracles, signs, and wonders Lord! Your kingdom is an everlasting kingdom of dominion and sovereign honor, that is being consumed and genetically established from generation to generation (Daniel 4:3, 7:14, 7:27)

THE HEAVENS DECLARE
YOUR GLORY

As *Kingdom Heirs*, one of the most important reasons we should desire to access and govern the heavens is so that the Lord can acquire glory out our lives. In order for this to occur continually, we must commune, align, and be intertwined with Him, His kingdom, His presence and His glory. Though the word says that Satan is the prince of the power of the air (*Ephesians 2:2*), he doesn't own the heavenlies. He doesn't own the second heavens, the sky, none of it. Actually when studying *Ephesians 2:2*, one will find that it is speaking about the sins of the world and how Satan is the ruler of the environment (air); he is orchestrator, agitator of the negative things within the world. This however, doesn't make Him prince of the heavenlies. Satan was cast down to earth (*Isaiah 14:12*) and that is all he has been given opportunity to wreak havoc over. When we look into the sky, nothing about it declares that Satan owns it. The sun, moon, stars, clouds, etc., all exude the creative beauty and glory of God. Even when it storms, snows, rains, etc., we are admonished by the declarative power of the Lord.

Psalms 19:1-6 asserts
(KJV)
The heavens declare the glory of God; and the firmament sheweth his handywork. Day unto day uttereth speech, and night unto night sheweth knowledge. There is no speech nor

language, where their voice is not heard. Their line is gone out through all the earth, and their words to the end of the world. In them hath he set a tabernacle for the sun, which is as a bridegroom coming out of his chamber, and rejoiceth as a strong man to run a race. His going forth is from the end of the heaven, and his circuit unto the ends of it:
and there is nothing hid from the heat thereof.

(Message)
God's glory is on tour in the skies, God-craft on exhibit across the horizon. Madame Day holds classes every morning, Professor Night lectures each evening. Their words aren't heard, their voices aren't recorded, but their silence fills the earth: unspoken truth is spoken everywhere. God makes a huge dome for the sun--a superdome! The morning sun's a new husband leaping from his honeymoon bed, The daybreaking sun an athlete racing to the tape. That's how God's Word vaults across the skies from sunrise to sunset, Melting ice, scorching deserts, warming hearts to faith.

Because many of us have not taken our rightful place within the heavenlies as *Kingdom Heirs*, Satan has put in systems to hinder and contend with us having direct access to our heavenly kingdom and even at times with the Lord.

Ephesians 6:12

(KJV)
For we wrestle not against flesh and blood, but against principalities, against powers, against

*the rulers of the darkness of this world, against
spiritual wickedness in high places.*

However, we discern from the very next passage of
scripture, that we have power to stand and be
victorious over the systems of Satan.

> *Verse 13-17(KJV)*
> *Wherefore take unto you the whole armour of
> God, that ye may be able to withstand in the evil
> day, and having done all, to stand. Stand
> therefore, having your loins girt about with
> truth, and having on the breastplate of
> righteousness; And your feet shod with the
> preparation of the gospel of peace; Above all,
> taking the shield of faith, wherewith ye shall be
> able to quench all the fiery darts of the wicked.
> And take the helmet of salvation, and the sword
> of the Spirit, which is the word of God:*

The word *Stand* in the *Greek* is *Histemi* and means:

1. to cause or make to stand, to place, put, set
2. to bid to stand by, [set up] in the presence of
    others, in the midst, before judges, before
    members of the Sanhedrin
3. to place, to make firm, fix establish
4. to cause a person or a thing to keep his or its
    place
5. to stand, be kept intact (of family, a kingdom),
    to escape in safety
6. to establish a thing, cause it to stand, to uphold
    or sustain the authority or force of anything

Our ability to stand denotes the establishment of the kingdom of heaven in the sphere to which we govern. When we stand our armor speaks for us. Just like the stars and the moon, etc., our armor represents the creative beauty of God's salvation, righteousness, truth, faith, peace and fashionably declares His Lordship over our lives and sphere of influence.

Psalms 50:6

(KJV)
And the heavens shall declare his righteousness: for God is judge himself. Selah.

(Amplified)
And the heavens declare His righteousness (rightness and justice), for God, He is judge. Selah [pause, and calmly think of that]!

(Message)
The whole cosmos attests to the fairness of this court, that here God is judge.

Psalms 97:1-2

(KJV)
The LORD reigneth; let the earth rejoice; let the multitude of isles be glad thereof. Clouds and darkness are round about him: righteousness and judgment are the habitation of his throne.

(NLT)
The LORD is king! Let the earth rejoice! Let the farthest coastlands be glad. Dark clouds

surround him. Righteousness and justice are the
foundation of his throne.

Often we are striving to resolve matters from an earthly sphere, but we simply are not of this world.

Philippians 3:20
(Amplified)
But we are citizens of the state (commonwealth, homeland) which is in heaven, and from it also we earnestly and patiently await [the coming of] the Lord Jesus Christ (the Messiah) [as] Savior.

(Message)
But there's far more to life for us. We're citizens of high heaven! We're waiting the arrival of the Savior, the Master, Jesus Christ.

John 15:19
(Amplified)
If you belonged to the world, the world would treat you with affection and would love you as its own. But because you are not of the world [no longer one with it], but I have chosen (selected) you out of the world, the world hates (detests) you.

(Message)
If you lived on the world's terms, the world would love you as one of its own. But since I picked you to live on God's terms

When we handle challenges from our homeland, and God's judgment is released, our very lives begin to declare God's justice and rightness. We are in turn activating our world and law and it is thus overriding the earthly world and law, while His will prevails on our behalf.

MY LIFE DECLARE HIS GLORY

1. The heavens are declaring God's glory and spewing forth His handiwork on my behalf and all that concerns me and His kingdom (Psalms 19:1).

2. Day by Day, my life is boasting among the Heavenlies that God is judge, Ruler above all.

3. Even the very significance of the sun, moon, stars, clouds, speak forth with silent violence that the Lord unequivocally reigns and is the highest law!

4. And just as the skies are dressed in God's decree, I am fashioned in the creative power of the Lord. I am continuously bonded in the helmet of salvation, the breastplate of righteousness; loins of truth, the shield of faith and the gospel of peace.

5. I stand in His reign and decree that through Him I am victorious against flesh and blood, principalities, powers, the rulers of the darkness of this world, and spiritual wickedness in high places.

6. I do not live by the world terms, yet am dictated and established in the constitution of God.

7. As a citizen of heaven, I declare that the fairness of my God's heavenly courts is proclaiming my destiny and is overriding any verdict of destruction, murder, sabotage, frustration, tragedy, and disorder.

8. Nothing is hindering me from my God and His kingdom. We are one and are united in the festivities of His goodness.

9. His law is perfect converting my soul. His testimonies are sure, making that which is wise simple. His statutes are right, rejoicing the heart. His commandments are pure, enlightening the eyes, His reverence is uncontaminated and long lasting. His judgments are true and righteous altogether (Psalms 19:7-8).

10. With my total existence and all that concerns me, I am declaring the glory of the Lord. I am a representation of His miraculous handiwork!

UNCONCEALED GLORY

1. As a *Kingdom Heir,* I stand on Psalms 24 and declaratively pronounce that the earth is the Lord's, and the fullness thereof; the world, and all that dwell therein. Every existence was founded upon Your glory God..

2. Through the power and authority of Jesus Christ, I supernaturally activate all hidden glory, stagnate glory, and stale glory. For the glory of the Lord is to be revealed and even now, the earth is being filled with the knowledge of the glory of the Lord. I have been created for His glory (Isaiah 40:5, 43:7, Habakkuk 2:14).

3. Ezekiel 39:21 proclaims that *He will be honored and magnified among all of mankind. That at appointed times, He sets His glory even among the heaven, such that His judgment and justice may be executed and established.*

4. I therefore declare that the glory of the Lord is everywhere and exerting Isaiah 60:1, I spew kingly utterances charging all of creation to *"Arise!*
Shine! For the light has come and the glory of the Lord has risen upon thee."

5. Give unto the Lord the glory due unto His name. Ascribe to the Lord, O sons of the mighty, ascribe to the Lord glory and strength! Worship the Lord in the beauty of holiness, in holy array. Yield unto the Lord the glory due His name (Psalms 29:1-3).

6. For the Lord is a shield that surrounds and engulfs me. You are my glory Lord, the lifter of my head (Psalms 3:3).

7. I decree that You are my Sun and Shield; You bestow present grace and favor and future glory that yields honor, splendor, and heavenly bliss! No good things are You withholding from me because I walk up rightly and are encompassed inside Your glory (Psalms 84:11).

8. Even as I birth forth Your kingdom, Your glory shines round about me as it did Mary when she was giving birth to Jesus (Luke 2:9).

9. Your glory releases specific keys that cover me, protect me, while leading me into destiny, fruitfulness, the fullness of Your promise land.

10. Within Your glory is guidance and direction...like a cloud guiding me by day and a pillar of fire by night (Exodus 34:15-23

11. You spread a cloud for a covering, and fire to give light by night. You, Father, spread out a cloud of glory as a protective covering and a fire to light up my dark challenging life experiences...releasing power and victory to contentious nights (Psalms 105:39).

12. For the spirit of glory and of God rests upon me. (1 Peter 4:14).

13. You are like a bubbly cheerful King, giving life, and Your favor is as a cloud bringing spring rain, restoring the latter rain unto me, the latter glory rain (Proverb 16:15).

14. As a *Kingdom Heir*, I search out Your glory and decree an unsealing of the matters of Your heart so that I can cultivate more glory for Your glory (Proverbs 25:2).

15. You, Father of glory, infuse me with the spirit of wisdom and revelation to know You more. You enlighten the eyes of my understanding that I may know the hope of my calling and receive understanding of the riches of the glory of my inheritance (Ephesians 1:17-18).

16. You have made me a little lower than the angels and have crowned me with glory, while giving me dominion over the works of Your hands, placing all things under my feet (Psalms 8:5-8).

17. You show me the path of life. A path full of Your presence, full of Your glory. For in Your presence is fullness of joy and at Your right hand are pleasures for evermore (Psalms 16:9).

18. I am swarmed by Your pleasures, being fashioned inside Your likeness. My life is constantly transformed and revealed as I am consumed to carry and wear Your glory (2Corinthians 3:18)

19. Blessed is God, the God of all! The one and only wonder-working God!
Blessed always is His blazing glory! All earth brims with His glory (Psalms 72:19)

20. Just as Jesus constantly stated, I exist to unseal glory for His glory (John 8:50).

INSIDE OF YOU

One morning during prayer, I had a vision where I went inside the chest of God and just abided there. It literally felt and looked like a hole inside the very body of the Lord and I fit perfectly inside Him. I prayed from this place. I roared, warred, declared, praised and worshipped, and rested from this place. It was comforting and replenishing all at the same time. The Lord told me that this place was always accessible to me and then gave me the scripture *Psalms 91:1-2,*

> *(KJV)*
> *He that dwelleth in the secret place of the most High shall abide under the shadow of the Almighty. I will say of the LORD, He is my refuge (shelter) and my fortress (stronghold, castle, fort) my God; in him will I trust.*

This passage of scripture is full of key words that fortify the importance and fruit of abiding in the Lord.

<u>Dwelleth</u> is *Yasab* and means:
1. to dwell, remain, sit, abide, to sit, sit down,
2. to be set, to remain, stay, have one's abode, to be inhabited,
3. a place, to cause to sit, to cause to dwell,
4. to cause (cities) to be inhabited, to marry (give an dwelling to)

Secret is *Seter* in the Hebrew means:

1. protection, covering, shelter,
2. hiding place, secrecy, secret place

Abide is *Lyin* in the Hebrew and means:

1. to lodge, stop over, pass the night,
2. abide, remain, to cause to rest, to dwell

Shadow is *Sel* in the Hebrew and means:

1. defense, shade, shadow, protection

Refuge is *Maha seh* in the Hebrew and means:

1. shelter, hope, trust, refuge
2. shelter from rain or storm, from danger, of falsehood (literally and figuratively)

(Amplified)
He who dwells in the secret place of the Most High shall remain stable and fixed under the shadow of the Almighty [Whose power no foe can withstand]. I will say of the Lord, He is my Refuge and my Fortress, my God; on Him I lean and rely, and in Him I [confidently] trust!

(Message)
You who sit down in the High God's presence, spend the night in Shaddai's shadow, Say this: "GOD, you're my refuge. I trust in you and I'm safe!"

(NLT)
Those who live in the shelter of the Most High will find rest in the shadow of the Almighty. This I

declare about the LORD: He alone is my refuge, my place of safety; he is my God, and I trust him.

The Lord took me deeper inside Him. He literally was telling me to come in and He was guiding me inward. There was open space and opportunity, and the Lord said everything you need is inside of me. He just kept saying that. I asked how do I obtain it and He said, "it's already yours" and I then heard "**John 15**."

> *(KJV)*
> *Verse 4-8*
> *Dwell in Me, and I will dwell in you. [Live in Me, and I will live in you.] Just as no branch can bear fruit of itself without abiding in (being vitally united to) the vine, neither can you bear fruit unless you abide in Me. I am the Vine; you are the branches. Whoever lives in Me and I in him bears much (abundant) fruit. However, apart from Me [cut off from vital union with Me] you can do nothing. If a person does not dwell in Me, he is thrown out like a [broken-off] branch, and withers; such branches are gathered up and thrown into the fire, and they are burned. If you live in Me [abide vitally united to Me] and My words remain in you and continue to live in your hearts, ask whatever you will, and it shall be done for you. When you bear (produce) much fruit, My Father is honored and glorified, and you show and prove yourselves to be true followers of Mine.*
> *(Message)*
> *"Live in me. Make your home in me just as I do in you. In the same way that a branch can't bear*

grapes by itself but only by being joined to the vine, you can't bear fruit unless you are joined with me. "I am the Vine, you are the branches. When you're joined with me and I with you, the relation intimate and organic, the harvest is sure to be abundant. Separated, you can't produce a thing. Anyone who separates from me is deadwood, gathered up and thrown on the bonfire. But if you make yourselves at home with me and my words are at home in you, you can be sure that whatever you ask will be listened to and acted upon. This is how my Father shows who he is--when you produce grapes, when you mature as my disciples.

<u>Abide</u> in the Greek is *Menoto* and means:

1. to stay (in a given place, state, relation or expectancy)
2. abide, continue, dwell, endure, be present, remain, stand, live
3. tarry, to sojourn, not to depart, to continue to be present
4. to be held, kept, continually, in reference to time, to continue to be
5. not to perish, to last, endure, to survive, to remain as one, not to become another or different

Abiding constitutes a continual dwelling in the Lord. It's a constant connection that allows us to be eternally connected to the Lord. We often hear preachers speak on this passage of scripture and I myself have studied it countless times, yet it often feels unattainable, especially when the cares and distractions of our earthly lives make God feel distant and callous. I asked the Lord one day what was the difference between being in Him and in heaven. The Lord said that heaven has everything earth could want, but inside of Him resides His literal essence. He said that heaven is like earth, it is its own little world, but inside of Him is His literal DNA. Heaven has to be accessed and applied but being inside of Him, makes whatever you need tangible and readily available. As I continue to experience God in this manner, I have learned that it is the place where our very character and image is transformed and built up in the Lord. Since He is the vine and we are the branches, we are extensions of Him, of who He is, of what He stands for. Dwelling inside of Him provides the attributes and tools necessary for governing our heavenly position through God's integrity and character. The more we enter this place, the more we begin to bear and exude the fruit and produce of God. And just like the stars and the moon, even without saying a word, our very existence declares His glory.

MY ETERNAL DWELLING PLACE
JESUS
(Inspired by Psalms 84)

1. The Amplified version of Psalms 84 declares, *How lovely are Your tabernacles, Your dwelling place, Oh Lord of hosts! My soul yearn, yes, even faint and is homesick for Your courts Oh Lord; my heart and flesh cry out and sing for joy to You the living God. Yes, the sparrow has found a house and the swallow a nest for herself, where she may lay her young – so I lay upon Your altars, Oh Lord of hosts, my King and my God. Blessed (happy, fortunate, to be envied) am I who dwell in Your house, swallowed in Your presence; I sing Your praises all the day long. Selah [pause, and calmly think of that]! Blessed (happy, fortunate, to be envied) am I because my strength is in You, my heart is the highway to You Oh Lord (Amplified).*

2. The Message Version of Psalms 84 declares, *what a beautiful home, God of the Angel Armies! I've always longed to live in a place like this, Always dreamed of a room in your house, inside your dwelling, where I could sing for joy to my God-alive! Birds find nooks and crannies in Your house; sparrows and swallows make nests there. They lay their eggs and raise their young, singing their songs in the place where I worship. God of the Angel Armies! My King! My God! How blessed I am to live and sing inside of You! How blessed am I to live, to abide continually inside of You.*

3. I further declare Psalms 55:1-5 which states, *For You Oh Lord are my light and my salvation; whom shall I fear? You are the strength of my life; of whom*

shall I be afraid? When the wicked, even my enemies and my foes, come upon us to eat up my flesh, they stumble and fall. Though a host encamps against me, my heart does not fear: though war rise against me, in this I am confident. One thing have I desired of You Oh Lord, that will I seek after; that I may dwell in the house of You Lord all the days of my life, to behold Your beauty, and to enquire in Your temple. For in the time of trouble You shall hide me in Your pavilion: in the secret of Your tabernacle shall You hide me; You shall set me up upon a rock. And now shall my head be lifted up above my enemies round about me: therefore will I offer in Your tabernacle sacrifices of joy; I will sing and worship and bow before You. Yea, I will release in bellows, praises unto You and on the behalf of Your kingdom Lord.

4. For I decree that inside of You is where I belong. For better is one day spent inside the very essence of You, a beautiful place of worship and refuge, than a thousand anywhere else Lord.

5. I decree that I abide here. I live here Lord. I am the branch of Your vine and my DNA is the very make up of Your presence.

6. My cells are infused with Your cells. My blood is transfused by the perfected blood of You Jesus. It is in You that I am moving, shifting, shaking....that I am breathing and releasing eternal abundant life and freely giving and establishing in others, all that is imparted and activated in me (Acts 17:28).

7. You are making me Your prototype, a very photocopy image of Your standard…a replica

of the likeness and fullness of what You have certified as good Jesus. We are good because we are Yours (Genesis 1:31).

8. Jesus You are the blueprint for how I have fruitful dominion, am to reproduce, subdue and fill the earth. I am eternally impacting and strategically successful in all that I apply my hands to do (Genesis 1:28).

9. I bless You for instilling the authority to multiply You in and through us, for You have scripted this charge into my being: I reign in the strength of John 14:12 which contends that *Greater works than these I will do. Greater works than the miracles, signs and wonders You did when You walked the earth, will I do emphatically for You* (John14:12).

10. As I abide in Your secret place, my communing is now becoming public declaration that I have not only been sojourning with You but am one with You.

11. My life is blessed as I live in You and conduct and project my life outwardly through You.

12. My strength is bold; my might is bountiful; my praise is monstrous, as I are consumed and delegated by Your inward truth.

13. There is death defying shelter here from every storm; protection from danger and falsehoods. Even in trying times, I go from strength to strength, as Your miraculous reveals that I live in the existence of Your fruit.

14. I rest in awe as I gaze upon Your salvation radiating fullness in my life. I stand afar and

laugh at the enemy licking my dust as He is unable to get to me....I am with You (Psalms 72:9).

15. I receive Your refuge Jesus and bless You that Your wings are a very fort for me. You are my lifestyle…my continual wealth for living…my tent of dwelling.

16. Even now I journey deeper inside of You. In deeper depth, I explore You. I come into deeper revelation and understanding of my relationship and covenant with You.

17. I am not blind or dull of hearing, for the eyes of my understanding are being enlightened as I behold You.

18. It is healing here and I absorb it. It is deliverance here and I devour it. I keep seeking You and I keep finding You pursuing me....our heartbeat synchronizing in divine harmony. I do as Amos 5:4 says, *I seek and live.* I seek and I are supernaturally charged. I seek and inquire of You as I require food. I seek and I am renovated, rejuvenated, revive, as I realize this is the only way to exist. I live right here in Your midst.

19. Your dwelling is the feast of life, my eternal tent of meeting. I reverence You Jesus as I discern the honor of being complete in You. The honor of indulging in the endless pleasures of Your glory light of truth. You Lord are my safe passage, my revelation for living; my eternal dwelling place.

I SOAK IN YOUR REST

1. I pursue the blessings of Psalms 42:1-2 and declare *that as the deer pants after the water brooks, so pants my souls after You, Oh God. My soul thirsts for You - for the one and only living God: when shall I come and appear before You, to drink deep gulps of Your presence? I am thirsty and longing for Godalive, thirsty to soak in the tranquil rest of my all powerful God.*

2. Hear, Oh Lord, when I cry distinctively the wealth of Psalms 27:7-14. *Have mercy upon me, and answer me. When You said, Seek Your face; my heart said unto thee, Your face, Oh Lord, will I seek. Hide not Your face far from me; put not Your servant away in anger: You have been my help; leave me not, neither forsake me, Oh God of my salvation. When my father and my mother forsake me, You Oh Lord, take me up. Teach me Your way, Oh Lord, and lead me in a plain path, because of my enemies. Deliver me not over unto the will of my enemies, for false witnesses rise up against me, and such as breathe out cruelty. I stand strong and unshaken because I believe I will see*
    Your goodness in the land of the living. Therefore, I wait on You Lord. I decree I have good courage, and receive fervently, the strengthening of my heart. I wait, I wait, I decree I am waiting and believing! I soak in the strength of waiting. I soak in the rest and refreshing of Your will and guidance as I wait on You Lord.

3. I pray into Psalms 121 and proclaim *that I am lifting up my eyes unto the hills, from which comes*

my help. My help is from You Lord. You made heaven and earth! You have not suffered my foot to be moved: I decree that my Guardian God slumbers not. He will not fall asleep. Behold, You watch over me and protect me; You Oh Lord are my shield and shelter! You Lord are the shade upon my right hand that keeps me from every evil and lurking enemy. Because of Your covering, the sun will not smite me by day, nor the moon by night. You preserve me from all maliciousness. You preserve my soul. The Lord has preserved my going out and my coming in from this time forth, and even for evermore.

4. I, in turn, soak in this sacred rest and decree that *the Lord is my shepherd; I shall not want. He makes me to lie down in green pastures. He leads me beside the still tranquil waters. He restores my soul. He leads me in the paths of righteousness for His name sake. Yea, though I walk through the valley of the shadow of death, I will fear no evil: I rest comfortably in my God, for You are with me; Your rod and Your staff, Oh Lord, they comfort me. You have prepared a table before me in the presence of my enemies. You anoint my head with oil; my cup runs over and over and over. Surely goodness and mercy is following me all the days of my life, and I decree that I dwell in the house of my Lord forever* (Psalms 23).

5. In this dwelling, resides a soaking rest. I have calmed and quieted my soul, like a weaned child with his mother, like a weaned child is my soul content within me. I've kept my feet on the ground. I've cultivated a quiet heart. Like a baby content in its mother's arms, my soul is a baby content. I wait, Oh I wait for You God. Waiting with hope. Hope now; hope always. I

hope while resting in the patience, timing, comfort and relationship with my God. (Psalm 131:2-3).

6. I meditate within my heart on my bed, and am still. I am quiet before Him. I am struck dumb in His rest (Psalm 4:4).

7. As I posture in stillness, the Lord provides me rest from all sorrow and pain, from trouble, unrest and from the responsibilities with which I have served for His glory (Isaiah 14:3).

8. You are mounting me up as I dismount and decrease before You, humbling beneath You. Your rest is giving me power in weak places and increasing my strength. I declare that as I put on Your strength I am increasing. As Your strength infuses me, I are making more strength. Even the youth shall faint and are weary, and the young men utterly fall, but because I wait on You Lord, You are renewing in abundance, my strength. I are mounting boldly, springing forth, shooting up, extending and ascending higher on kingly wings like an explosive eagle. I am running and dismantling weariness; I am walking and fainting not (Isaiah 40:29-31). Yes! Yes! I am refreshing in the power of the Lord.

9. Immersed in Your heavenly soaking, I lean in my Lord and fret not concerning the evil doers who appear to prosper despite their ways. (Psalm 37:7).

10. For I hear You quickening me, saying, "*Come to Me, my children who have been laboring and is*

heavy laden, and I will give you rest. Take My yoke upon you and learn from Me, for I am gentle and lowly in heart, and you will find rest for your soul. For My yoke is easy and My burden is light" (Matthew 11:28-30).

11. I take up Your yoke and rest. Yes, I release all the cares and trials of this world, and I rest.

12. I bless You Lord for delivering me out of the hand of the wicked, and redeeming me out of the hand of the terrible (Jeremiah 15:21).

13. I the righteous am delivered out of trouble (Proverbs 11:8).

14. As Your righteous, I have experienced many afflictions but You, Lord, have delivered me from them all (Psalms 34:19).

15. So I declare that my precious Lord has given me rest on every side, such that there is neither adversary nor evil impacting or challenging me. The Lord has provided peace all around me, no one against me, nothing at odds with me. (1Kings 5:4)

16. For within You remains a powerful consuming rest for Your people. I decree I have entered Your rest while ceasing from every work, even those that are good but not directed by You God. I am therefore, diligent to enter into Your secluded place of soaking rest (Hebrews 4:911).

17. Just like Mary, I sit at Your feet Jesus and hang onto Your every word, I rest (Luke 10:39).

18. I dwell safely because I listen to You Lord and You secure me without fear of evil. I pay attention to You and I relax. I take it easy in

You, believing wholeheartedly that all things are working together for my good. Surrendering to Your holy hush....I rest (Proverbs 1:33, Romans 6:28).

19. For You Oh Lord have allured me. You have brought me into the wilderness and speak comfort and guidance unto me (Hosea 2:14).

20. And within the virtue of Your rest, I seek Your kingdom, and all Your righteousness, trusting that everything I need is being added unto me (Matthew 6:33)

21. Even now, Your spirit Lord is resting upon me, the spirit of wisdom and understanding, the spirit of counsel and might, the spirit of knowledge and the reverential fear of my Lord (Isaiah 11:2).

22. I hope in You Lord: for I shall continually praise You. You are the deliverance, health and welfare of my countenance, and my God. The savior and victory of my life (Psalm 42:11).

23. I bathe in contentment and quietly rely and enter into Your trusted place of refreshing and renewal. My glory is fresh in me and my bow is renewed as I soak in the power of Your rest (Job 29:20).

SWEET HEAVENLY SLEEP

Often when the enemy can't overcome us in our daily lives, he will begin attacking us in the sleep realm. It's important to realize that the sleep realm is real. Life doesn't stop just because we are sleep. Our bodies take a break but the world, atmosphere and spirit realm around us is continuing to progress and evolve. The enemy tends to use the darkness, night time and even night seasons, to conjure and release his craftiest attacks against us. He knows that our defenses are at rest so he tries to take advantage of our need for sleep and refreshing. All through the bible God encouraged us to sleep and to rest. The Lord even sat aside a day of rest in which He called the —Sabbath‖ and encouraged us to keep it holy (Genesis 2:2, Exodus 23:12, Exodus 20:8). Jesus slept and rested (Matthew 8:24, Matthew 6:31). This alone lets us know that we are covered as we sleep and rest and do not have to be subjected to the night terrors of the enemy.

Psalms 91:1-8

(KJV)

He that dwelleth in the secret place of the most High shall abide under the shadow of the Almighty. I will say of the Lord, He is my refuge and my fortress: my God; in him will I trust. Surely he shall deliver thee from the snare of the fowler, and from the noisome pestilence. He shall cover thee with his feathers, and under his wings shalt thou trust: his truth shall be thy shield and buckler. Thou shalt not be afraid for the terror by night; nor for the arrow that flieth by day; Nor for the pestilence that walketh in darkness; nor for the destruction that wasteth at noonday. A thousand shall fall at thy side, and ten thousand at thy right hand; but it shall not come nigh thee. Only with thine eyes shalt thou behold and see the reward of the wicked.

Terror in *Hebrew* is *Pachad* and means:

1. a (sudden) alarm (properly, the object feared, by implication, the feeling)
2. dread(ful), fear, (thing) great (fear, feared), terror
3. terror, dreadful, greatly, object of dread

Merriam Webster's Online Dictionary defines *Terror*:

1. a state of intense fear
2. one that inspires fear, scourage
3. a frightening aspect, a cause of anxiety, worry, an appalling person or thing
4. reign or terror
5. violent or destructive acts (as bombing) committed by groups in order to intimidate a population or government into granting their demands

The things the enemy attempts to deposit when a person is sleeping are essentially the attributes of terror. The terrors of death, fear, sickness, tragedy, etc., are not just nightmares or demonic attacks, they are real demonic impartations meant to terrorize and wreak havoc in our lives. These demonic dreams and night visitors have the same assignment as the terrorists that blow up buildings with hundreds of people in them or as the terrorist that walk into a school and unload gun rounds on a classroom full of kids. Their assignment is to shock and terrorize to a degree that a person's life is altered from the fear, dread and death that has been unveiled.

Often it isn't enough to rebuke these nightmarish dreams and demonic night visitors. It is important to assert authority over them through intercession and warfare. When these dreams and demonic attacks are unchallenged, they pose the potential to manifest in a person's natural life. It isn't uncommon for someone to have a dream about someone dying and they die or having an accident and one occurs. And even if the dream experience itself doesn't come to pass, such dreams and encounters leave such negative deposits, that a person awakens exhausted, depressed, fearful, confused, appalled, drained, tired, grieved, manic, etc., among other things. The chilling effects of the terror, has infiltrated the person's mind, soul and emotions. This is because the sleep realm is alive; it's a real sphere of influence and thus the dreams and demonic encounters are alive and real.

SWEET SLEEP DECLARATION

Psalms 91

I dwell in the secret place of the most High and abide under the shadow of the Almighty. I say of LORD, You are my refuge and my fortress: my God; inYou I trust. Surely you have deliver me from the snare of the fowler, and from the noisome pestilence. You have covered me with You feathers, and under Your wings I do trust: Your truth is my shield and buckler. I am not afraid of the terror by night; nor for the arrow that flieth by day; Nor for the pestilence that walketh in darkness; nor for the destruction that wasteth at noonday. A thousand has fallen at my side, and ten thousand at my right hand; but it will not come nigh me. Only with my eyes do I behold and see the reward of the wicked.

Because I have made You LORD, which is my refuge, even the most High, my habitation; There shall no evil befall me, neither shall any plague come nigh my dwelling. For You Lord have given your angels charge over me, to keep me in all my ways. They bear me up in their hands, lest I dash my foot against a stone.

I tread upon the lion and adder: the young lion and the dragon I trample under feet. Because I hath set my love upon You God, You have delivered me: You have set me on high, because I know Your name. When I call upon You, You answer me: You have and will deliver me out of trouble; You have honored me and shown me the protection and covering of your salvation.

1. As a *Kingdom Heir,* I decree that I have power over all the power of the enemy whether awake, sleep, in my dreams, and within the spirit realm (Luke 10:19).

2. For I undoubtedly know that weapons of my warfare are not carnal, but mighty through God to the pulling down of strongholds. Even in my sleep, I cast down imaginations, and every high thing that exalts itself against the knowledge of God, and bring into captivity every thought, intent, devise, and action to the obedience of Christ (2Corinthians 10:4).

3. I decree I am well balanced, temperate, sober of mind, vigilant and cautious at all times, even when asleep; such that my enemy can't seize upon me to devour my destiny (1Peter 5:8).

4. I stand on Isaiah 54:17 and declare that no weapon that is formed against me shall prosper, in season or out of season, when I am sleep or in a place of rest; and contend that the Lord eternally condemns every tongue, instrument, and demonic entity that rise against me. This is my heritage because I am a servant of You, Lord.

5. I assert my God given authority as a *Kingdom Heir,* and decree a keen sensitivity to detect dangers seen and unseen. I decree that just as in everyday life, I have power to perpetually arrest, disrupt, and halt ungodly dreams and demonic attacks; even to the point of taking immediate authority within my dreams and the

spirit realm, while changing and shifting them to a place of deliverance, healing, and victory.

6. When I lie down, I am not afraid; yes, I shall lie down, and my sleep will be sweet. Whether asleep or awake, I am not afraid neither of sudden terror and panic, nor of stormy blasts or the storm and ruin of the wicked. For You Lord are my confidence, firm and strong, and You are keeping my destiny from being caught in demonic and soulish traps or hidden dangers of the enemy (Proverbs 3:23-26).

7. I repent for sins personally and generationally; sins committed in my household, upon my land, and sphere of influence. I close all doors spiritually and naturally to nightmares, generational idolatry, familiar spirits, night terrors, the boogieman, ghosts, invaders, feeders, perversion, rape, and molestation spirits, night visitors, witches, warlocks, astral projectors and demonic attackers, spirits of death and hell, demonic harassment and stranglers (Matthew 5:25).

8. I receive forgiveness and decree a freeing from all anxiousness, worry, fear, stress, anger, hatred, unforgiveness, uncleanness, trauma, etc., and decree a cleansing and freeing from any soulish and emotional areas that would give way to the enemy.

9. For I do not fret or have any anxiety about anything, but in every circumstance and in everything, by prayer and petition (definite requests), with thanksgiving, I continue to

make my wants known to my God. And my God's peace has become a tranquil state within my soul. I am assured of my salvation through Christ. And so fearing nothing and being content with my Kingly inheritance, I decree that His peace, which transcends all understanding is garrisoning and mounting a powerful guard over my heart and mind and is brooding wholeness and wellness in me. (Philippians 4:6-7).

10. I therefore cancel all dedications, covenants, rituals, hexes, vexes, enchantments, bewitchments made to demons and idols, witches, warlocks, wicked people, as it relates to me personally, generationally, my land and sphere of influence, and the spiritual gifts in my family lineage (Numbers 4:18).

11. I close every, door, gateway and portal, spiritually and naturally, to demonic dreams, astral projection and my spirit man being subjected to ungodly summons in the night. I fully resist the devil and decree I only harken to the unction and voice of my King Jesus (James 4:7).

12. I plead the blood of Jesus over me, my home, my bed, my covers, my atmosphere, my possessions and sphere of influence and decree that to the pure, in heart and conscience, all things are pure (Titus 1:15).

13. As born again *Kingdom Heir*, I decree I am covered by the purified blood of Jesus and solidified in the all-powerful name of Jesus - the

name that is above every name - the name to which every knee shall bow and every tongue should confess that My Jesus is Lord and savior unto the glory of God my Father, Refuge, Shelter, and Protector (Philippians 2:811).

14. Even now I cleanse my body, mind, spirit, soul, thoughts, emotions, personality, character, will, and sphere of influence of all tragedy, infirmity, affliction, fear, worry, weariness, tiredness, frustration, failure, depression, loneliness, double mindedness, unbelief, perversion, demonic seeds, pollution, imprints, impressions (*speak forth whatever negative attributes have been planted through dreams and demonic night attacks*). I decree a complete cleansing and healing through the blood of Jesus and the matchless name of Jesus and command every seed, root, manifestation, harvest, stench and stain of these ungodly attributes to be annulled. You are destroyed, rendered powerless and zapped to nothing by the declarative name of Jesus (Proverbs 23:7).

15. For there is no torment in love. God grants sleep to those He loves. I am consumed by God's perfect love which causes Him to sustain and comfort me as I sleep (1 John 4:18, Psalms 42:8, Psalms 127:2) 16. Angels are protecting and working on my behalf as I rest and sleep (Psalms 34:7, 91:11).

17. I decree that instead of demonic activity and hellish dreams, God instructs me in the night season (Psalm 16:7).

18. For it is God's desire for me to know the mysteries of the kingdom of heaven. I therefore declare that as I sleep, I shall not only awaken refreshed, but shall have prophetic dreams and visions and receive kingdom keys, strategies, and heavenly downloads from my God. These revelations shall expose the enemy, release answers, direction, cures, and understanding, change life, build faith, shift atmospheres, overtake regions, and produce and establish the glory of God in the earth (Matthew 13:11).

19. Even in my sleep, I take up the yoke of the Lord. Your yoke is comforting, delivering, healing, revitalizing, strengthening, empowering, elevating, activating and releasing fulfillment to my royal lineage and destiny (Matthew 11:28).

20. I shall arise proclaiming that my sleep was sweet, for I have been fruitfully blessed and nourished in sweet heavenly sleep (Jeremiah 31:26).

UNSHAKEABLE PEACE

John 16:33

(KJV)
These things I have spoken unto you, that in me ye might have peace. In the world ye shall have tribulation: but be of good cheer; I have overcome the world.

(Amplified)
I have told you these things, so that in Me you may have [perfect] peace and confidence. In the world you have tribulation and trials and distress and frustration; but be of good cheer [take courage; be confident, certain, undaunted]! For I have overcome the world. [I have deprived it of power to harm you and have conquered it for you.]

(Message)
I've told you all this so that trusting me, you will be unshakable and assured, deeply at peace. In this godless world you will continue to experience difficulties. But take heart! I've conquered the world."

In this scripture Jesus is speaking to the disciples about His time nearing for being sacrificed on the cross for all of mankind. Jesus stated that He was sharing this revelation with them so that they would have perfect unshakable peace when chaos begins to unfold in His midst. Even though Jesus hadn't yet died and resurrected, He told the disciples not to fear the world and the tribulations that would occur, for He had already overcome the world.

Overcome is *Nikao* in the Greek and means:
1. to subdue, prevail, to carry off the victory, come off victorious
2. conquer, to carry off the victory, come off victorious
3. of Christ, victorious over all His foes
4. of Christians, that hold fast their faith even unto death against the power of their foes, and temptations and persecutions
5. when one is arraigned or goes to law, to win the case, maintain one's cause

Jesus understood that His life was truly about walking out (producing judgment) in the natural, what had already manifested in the spirit. In the spirit realm He had already overcome the world; subdued it and walked in dominion. He lived from the perspective that His destiny was already fulfilled and therefore, despite worldly trials, He existed from His state of heavenly peace. He lived from His heavenly kingdom and never allowed being born into the world and journeying among the world, to shift Him into the world's tribulations and frenzies. He didn't allow the world to draw Him from the peace and power to which He possessed within His heavenly standard of living and existing.

Peace in this scripture is translated *Eirene* and means:

1. prosperity, quietness, rest, set at one again
2. a state of national tranquility
3. exemption from the rage and havoc of war
4. peace between individuals, harmony, concord
5. security, safety, prosperity, felicity, (because peace and harmony make and keep things safe and prosperous)
6. of the Messiah's peace, the way that leads to peace (salvation), of Christianity,
7. the tranquil state of a soul assured of its salvation through Christ, and so fearing nothing from God and content with its earthly lot, of whatsoever sort that is
8. the blessed state of devout and upright men after death

Peace in Merriam Webster's Online dictionary means:

1. a state of tranquility or quiet, a freedom from civil disturbance
2. state of security or order within a community provided for by law or custom
3. freedom from disquieting or oppressive thoughts or emotions harmony in personal relations
4. a state or period of mutual concord between governments

5. a pact or agreement to end hostilities between those who have been at war or in a state of enmity used interjectionally to ask for silence or calm or as a greeting or farewell

6. in a state of concord or tranquility, in a state without war

7. accord, amity, concord, harmony; calm, quiet, serenity, tranquility; order, stability; pacification

The tribulations of this world are sent to cause trouble, affliction, fear, persecution, anguish, ungodly burden, distress, pressure, oppression, etc. Jesus says in *John 14:27,*

> *(KJV)*
> *Peace I leave with you, my peace I give unto you: not as the world giveth, give I unto you. Let not your heart be troubled, neither let it be afraid.*

> *(Amplified)*
> *Peace I leave with you; My [own] peace I now give and bequeath (pass down) to you. Not as the world gives do I give to you. Do not let your hearts be troubled, neither let them be afraid. [Stop allowing yourselves to be agitated and disturbed; and do not permit yourselves to be fearful and intimidated and cowardly and unsettled.]*

> *(Message)*
> *I'm leaving you well and whole. That's my parting gift to you. Peace. I don't leave you the*

*way you're used to being left--feeling abandoned,
bereft. So don't be upset. Don't be distraught.*

Jesus makes it clear that the peace He gives comes
directly from Him. It isn't a temporary peace or a
conditional peace. But it is a lifestyle that produces
a wellness and wholeness. Jesus contends that it is
the world that is attempting to dispel true peace.
We can assume from what He is saying that our
very nature and sphere of influence as *Kingdom
Heirs* is in a state of heavenly peace. It already
exists, yet when we are swayed and impacted by
the world the truth of our reality is altered by the
world's reality. This is the reason Jesus was able to
sleep during the great storm while the disciples
panicked and feared for their lives.

Mark 4:36-41

(KJV)

*And when they had sent away the multitude,
they took him even as he was in the ship. And
there were also with him other little ships. And
there arose a great storm of wind, and the waves
beat into the ship, so that it was now full. And
he was in the hinder part of the ship, asleep on a
pillow: and they awake him, and say unto him,
Master, carest thou not that we perish? And he
arose, and rebuked the wind, and said unto the
sea, Peace, be still. And the wind ceased, and
there was a great calm. And he said unto them,
Why are ye so fearful? how is it that ye have no
faith? And they feared exceedingly, and said one
to another, What manner of man is this, that
even the wind and the sea obey him?*

Jesus never allowed what was occurring around Him to sway Him from His true reality as a heavenly being. When we grasp this revelation, we can remain in a place of divine peace and rest no matter what trials manifest in our lives. We understand our purpose and destiny and can live from that place of destiny. In living in this kingly position, we can manifest our heavenly world around us while the earthly world is in discord and havoc.

PEACE! NOT AS THE WORLD GIVES

1. I the name of Jesus, decree that I receive my heavenly reality of unshakable peace from You, Jesus. Peace! Not as the world gives. But peace that comes from the very DNA of my heavenly home (John 14:27).

2. As a *Kingdom Heir,* I thank You for imparting Your peace into me, for leaving it with me, and for encouraging me to embrace the power, authority, aroma, nature and heavenly reality of peace.

3. I reject the trials and tribulations of this world. Even when challenging situations occur, I remain in a tranquil state of peace.

4. I continually seek You for my purposed destiny and I am open to walking out naturally what has already occurred in the spirit realm. I say burdens, oppression, and mental anguish are not my lot. And even when being persecuted for righteousness sake, I remained grounded in the purpose of my destiny. I remained consecrated in the vigor of peace.

5. For You, Christ Jesus have continuously reminded me and demonstrated through the fulfillment of Your work at the cross, that the world has been conquered. As a *Kingdom Heir, I,* too, have subdued, prevailed, overcome and conquered this world.

6. I am victorious and assert my victory! I decree I am more than conquerors through Christ Jesus who loves us. *I am uncompromisingly persuaded beyond a doubt (am sure) that neither death nor life, nor angels nor principalities, nor things impending and threatening nor things to come, nor powers, nor height nor depth, nor anything else in all creation will be able to separate me from the love of God which is in Christ Jesus my Lord* (Romans 8:38-39).

7. Though the enemy devises his strategies, they are thwarted. He proposes his plans, yet they will not stand. I rebuke the strategies of the enemy while declaring exemption from rage of demonic havoc and war. I spew out peace!

8. God thwarts the plans of the crafty so that their hands achieve no success, for God is with me. He has given me complete, sound, surpassing peace. Such peace yields a state of security and order in my sphere of influence...harmonizing all that concerns me (Job 5:12, Isa 8:10).

9. Plan and plot all you want--nothing will prosper. All your talk is mere babble, empty words with no fruit; because when all is said and done, the last word is Immanuel--God-With-Us. He is my voice, my reality, my temperament, my peace.

10. Call your councils of war, but they will be worthless. Develop your strategies, but they will not succeed. For God is with me! I still myself in the call to trust the Lord, I still the storms of life with my validity of peace (Isa 8:10).

11. In Jesus name, I call forth a mutual concord of agreement between my heavenly government and the government of this world. I declare silence upon the hostilities that attempts to steal, destroy, dismantle and displace the calm felicity of my assertive peace.

12. For You Lord, have ordained, orchestrated, delegated, and declared the judgment and laws of my surroundings. I am established in Your peace (Isaiah 26:12).

13. You guard me and keep me in perfect and constant peace because my mind - both its inclination and its character – stays centered in You; I am committed to You, lean on You and hope confidently in You (Isaiah 26: 3).

14. Your peace is a fruitful weapon that proclaims my spiritual supremacy.
    It isn't conditional, flawed, empty or temporary, like the world gives. It
    is a silent vengeance evaporating the wretched storm. I declare Your supernatural gift of peace.

KINGLY DESTINY

Jeremiah 29:11-14:

> *(KJV)*
>
> *For I know the thoughts that I think toward you, saith the LORD, thoughts of peace, and not of evil, to give you an expected end. Then shall ye call upon me, and ye shall go and pray unto me, and I will hearken unto you. And ye shall seek me, and find me, when ye shall search for me with all your heart. And I will be found of you, saith the LORD: and I will turn away your captivity, and I will gather you from all the nations, and from all the places whither I have driven you, saith the LORD; and I will bring you again into the place whence I caused you to be carried away captive.*

Thoughts in the Hebrew is *Machashabah* and means:

1. thought, device, purpose
2. work, imaginations, cunning,
3. something devised, invented, an invention

The thoughts that God has are not just random thoughts. They are specific and strategic thoughts that aide in assisting us in getting to purposed destinations so our destiny can be revealed. One of the definitions of the word *thoughts* is *device*.

Device in Merriam-Webster's Online Dictionary means:

1. a thing made for a particular purpose; an invention or contrivance, especially a mechanical or electrical one

2. a plan or scheme for effecting a purpose

3. a crafty scheme; trick

4. a particular word pattern, figure of speech, combination of word sounds, etc., used in a literary work to evoke a desired effect or arouse a desired reaction in the reader: rhetorical devices

5. something elaborately or fancifully designed

6. a representation or design used as a heraldic charge or as an emblem, badge, trademark, or the like

7. a motto

<u>*Motto* in Merriam-Webster's Online Dictionary means:</u>

1. a maxim adopted as an expression of the guiding principle of a person, organization, city, etc.

2. a sentence, phrase, or word expressing the spirit or purpose of a person, organization, city, etc., and often inscribed on a badge, banner, etc.

It is import to ask the Lord, "What's my motto." What's that specific device that defines me as Your *Kingdom Heir.* This key is essential in establishing the path and direction of journeying into your destiny.

The Hebrew definition says that the thoughts God has towards us are already invented...it's an invention. God's thoughts aren't being invented or will be invented...they have already been devised for us, which means His thoughts have already come to pass. There is already a pattern in the Spirit for what God has created, ordained and designed us to be and do. Our motto (banner) has already manifested spiritually, we just have to take our rightful place as heirs to be strategically aligned with manifesting our destiny naturally. Message Version of *Jeremiah 29:11-14* states:

> *I know what I'm doing. I have it all planned out--plans to take care of you, not abandon you, plans to give you the future you hope for. "When you call on me, when you come and pray to me, I'll listen. "When you come looking for me, you'll find me. "Yes, when you get serious about finding me and want it more than anything else, I'll make sure you won't be disappointed." GOD's Decree. "I'll turn things around for you. I'll bring you back from all the countries into which I drove you"--GOD's Decree--"bring you home to the place from which I sent you off into exile. You can count on it.*

Expected end is one that is hoped for...longed for! Everything you have hoped for has already been designed to manifest for you (WHEWWWWW)! The word —End" in this scripture doesn't mean it's over. Many of you think that because you have made mistakes, have gotten off track, have aged, that your destiny is over. God was letting His people know in this passage of scripture that though they would go into captivity for a time, it wasn't over. There is an appointed time of deliverance for them.

<u>*End* in the Hebrew is *Achar* and means:</u>
1. after the following part, behind (of place)
2. hinder, hinder part, afterwards (of time)

God has already set it up where even if one gets off track, he or she has the opportunity to realign with his or her destiny....that even in captivity, destiny can emerge from it. The important fact in this scripture that God revealed was that it was important that people knew His plans. If you read chapter 29 of Jeremiah, you will discern that the people had been listening to false prophets and voices that weren't speaking the word and will of the Lord. God didn't want the people to be ignorant so He told Jeremiah to release His word as it would expose the words of error and set the nation on course for being realigned with Him. That though they would indeed experience captivity because of past sins, there would be a specific time of being restored in the things of the Lord.   Ascend to a posture of hearing your Kingly motto and receive the thoughts, devices, inventions of the Lord for your life that will birth forth your destiny.

DESTINY MOTTO! MY PATH OF LIFE

1. Thank You Lord for my life's purpose that is destined for success and greatness.

2. For You Oh Lord shaped me first inside, then out; You formed me in my mother's womb. You Oh Lord do nothing happenstance or without intentions. Your hand, wisdom, and guidance is in every fiber of my existence (Psalms 139).

3. You Lord know me better than I know myself, I decree my destiny and the destiny of all that concerns me is in Your hands. I release it totally to You and seek You for Your will and path for my Life. You Oh Lord, are a lamp unto my feet and light unto my path (Psalms 119:105).

4. For Job 26:11 contends that if I obey and serve You, I will spend my days in prosperity and my years in contentment.

5. You fill my mouth with laughter and my lips with shouts of joy (Job 8:21).

6. You cover me with Your feather, shelter me with Your wings; Your faithful promises are my armor and protection (Psalms 91:4).

7. I therefore, relinquish my destiny to You and come into agreement with the thoughts, intents, devices, inventions that You have regarding me. Thoughts of peace and not of evil, to give me an expected hope and future (Jeremiah 29:11).

8. I decree Your thoughts are my motto, my banner; Your thoughts are what transcribes, embodies, inspires...pilots my journey.

9. All other thoughts, devices, mottos, plans, are cancelled in the name of Jesus and are disengaged from my life and lineage.

10. For You Lord know what You are doing. You know what You have planned. Even if captivity falls upon me, when I call upon You in a seek, You will listen and come looking for me. You will make sure I am not disappointed as this is Your decree to me from the scriptures. You will turn things around for me and bring me back into the place of which I was driven. You will bring me home to the place from which I was exiled...In my repentance, wearing Your grace, I am never exiled from You; I can count on Your forgiveness and restoration...Your times of refreshing as it is Your written decree for my destiny (Jeremiah 29:1114, Acts 3:19).

11. Even now I proclaim that You Oh Lord, are releasing that refreshing of the former rain in just measure and in righteousness, the former and the latter rain. For as a Kingdom Heir, I call forth the restoration of past seasons of captivity. I declare even now that You have forgiven me and my lineage; You are thus restoring my threshing floors with grain, my vats with an overflow of wine and oil. You Oh Lord are reestablishing the years that the locust

has eaten—the hopping locust, the stripping locust, and the crawling locust (Joel 2:22-25).

12. Restoration and alignment is being restored to every place within the path of my destiny.

    ☐ LORD my God, you have performed many wonders for me and all that concerns me. Your plans for me and mines are too numerous to list. You have no equal. If I tried to recite all Your wonderful deeds, I would never come to the end of them (Psalms 40:5).

13. Your words Lord regarding me are sure and true. They do not return unto You empty; They accomplish that which You purpose, and succeed in the thing for which You sent them (Isaiah 55:11).

14. For still the vision awaits its appointed time; it aches for its coming, it hastens to the end—it will not lie. If it seems slow, I wait for it; it will surely come; it will not delay. God is not a man that He would lie. Every word and vision He has for me will come right on time (Habakkuk 2:3, Numbers 23:19).

15. I do not forsake the works of God's hands in my life for His steadfast love and mercy endures forever. With intense sensitive workings, God is perfecting everything which concerns me (Psalms 138:8).

16. God declared the end from the beginning and prophesied ancient times things not yet done. His counsel stands, thus His will and purpose

for me is a done deal. It will be accomplished (Isaiah 46:10).

17. I therefore, take no thought for tomorrow, for tomorrow is already destined and is taking care of itself (Matthew 6:34).

18. All things are working together for my good and are fitting into God's plan for me because I love God and have been called according to His purpose (Romans 8:28).

19. In the victory and strength of my destiny motto, I'm off and running; I'm not turning back. Solidified in the thoughts, words, devices, inventions of God, I press productively towards the prize of the high calling of Christ (Philippians 3:14)

20. I shall live and not die to declare the works of the Lord (Psalms 118:17).

KINGLY TRANSFORMATION

Romans 12:2

(KJV)
I are not conformed to this world: but are transformed (transfigured, changed into another formed) by the renewing (renovation, changed for the better) of my minds, that I may prove what is that good, and acceptable, and perfect, will of God.

(Amplified)
I are not conformed to this world (this age), [fashioned after and adapted to its external, superficial customs], but I are transformed (changed) by the [entire] renewal of my mind [by its new ideals and its new attitude], so that I may prove [for ourselves] what is the good and acceptable and perfect will of God, even the thing which is good and acceptable and perfect [in His sight for us].

(Message)
I will not become so well-adjusted to my culture that I fit into it without even thinking. Instead, I fix my attention on God. This will change us from the inside out. I readily recognize what He wants from us, and quickly respond to it. Unlike the culture around us, always dragging us down to its level of immaturity, God brings the best out of us, develops well-formed maturity in us.

1. I declare a shift in my mind today! A shift in my life today! A shift in my lineage today! A

shift of transformation today! Old things are cast off, all things become new. No more mediocre progress! Come heaven's instant renovating change! Transfigure me into God's perfected truth (2Corinthians 5:17).

2. For I decree that because Jesus Christ has set me free, I am free indeed. Not by my works, but at His cost and heaven's gain, I have been granted a freebie (John 8:36).

3. I stand fast in the liberty that Christ has made me free, and declare that from this day forward, I am no longer entangled with the lies and deeds of this world, the evil yoke of bondage, no more a slave to sin, death and hell...no more am I constrained by the demonic wiles that hinder me from receiving God's resuscitating love. I am free! I am changing! Kingly transformation is taking place in me (Galatians 5:1).

4. For I have not only received the truth of my Lord and Savior Jesus Christ, but I know the truth and His truth has set me free (John 8:32).

5. I assert His word which declares that where the spirit of the Lord is, there is liberty. His Spirit is what guides, comforts, teaches, empowers – with kingly privilege He redefines my very nature and presentation.
Christ through His Spirit is a living dwelling place within my being. (2Corinthians 3:17).

6. For as in Adam all die, yet in Christ, all are made alive (1Corinthians 15:22).

7. Thanks be to God, who always cause me to triumph and leads me to spread everywhere the fragrance of the knowledge of Jesus Christ. I say! I declare! I leave the aroma of Christ everywhere. (2 Corinthians 2:14).

8. For though I am not yet perfect, I am surrendered, and He is perfecting those things which concern me (Psalms 138:8).

9. I am confident of this very thing that He who has begun a good work in me is performing it and will continue until the day of Jesus Christ. What's impossible with man, is possible with God, through Him I leave an eternal legacy for others to reap from and live by (Luke 18:27, Philippians 1:6).

10. I am continually changing, never the same; as with an open face I am beholding like in a glass, the glory of the Lord. And He is changing me into His image, His likeness, an ever increasing transformation, from level to level, glory to glory; my soul and mind is being cultivated and established on things that fulfill....things above this world (2Corinthians 3:18, Colossians 3:2)

11. For Jesus has redeemed me from the curse of the law, being made a curse for us: for it is written, cursed is every one that hangs on a tree (Galatians 3:13)

12. I have been justified freely by His grace through the redemption of His blood, cross, resurrection...raised and rebirth anew....Blessings of the Lord rain your mercies upon me (Romans 3:24, Ephesians 1:7).

13. I look unto Jesus only, the author and perfection of my faith (Hebrews 12:2).

14. I praise you recklessly; for I am fearfully and wonderfully made.(Psalms 139:13)

15. And so I reject the dragging down of this world, Spirit to Spirit, I commune and receive only that which is of my God (John 4:24)

16. I am kingly transformed, fashioned by His armor, His fads and latest style. I stand declaring and infiltrating life's very existence, with the salvation, righteousness, truth, peace, beauty, and holiness of my God with fervent intentions (Romans 13:14, Ephesians 6).

17. **I DECLARE MY KINGLY TRANSFORMATION!**

THE ROYAL SEED

Often there are spirits within the family line that are used to destroy the royalty that God has designed for that lineage.

2Kings 11:1-3
> *(KJV)*
> *And when Athaliah the mother of Ahaziah saw that her son was dead, she arose and destroyed all the seed royal. But Jehosheba, the daughter of king Joram, sister of Ahaziah, took Joash the son of Ahaziah, and stole him from among the king's sons which were slain; and they hid him, even him and his nurse, in the bedchamber from Athaliah, so that he was not slain. And he was with her hid in the house of the LORD six years. And Athaliah did reign over the land for six years.*

The manners in which I have seen the spirit of Athaliah operate is that it will use a person to kill several family members or a group of people, then have the person kill him or herself. I have also discerned that this spirit will reside within a family line, and then will begin to kill off the royal seeds whether spiritually or naturally, in effort to assert control and power over the lineage. This spirit manifests and attacks as a genocide within the family line. It usually operates in idolatry, lacks remorse for his or her actions, and will use witchcraft, manipulation, and demonic legalism to gain authority over those around them.

Often we allow this spirit to hang out in our family because after all it is operating as our mother, father, cousin, aunt, grandma, etc. This spirit is often passed down from generation from generation because those within the family line do not expose this spirit for what it is due to respecting the person who is oppressed or possessed with it. We see this with Athaliah as she was the daughter of King Ahab of Israel and his Baal-worshipping wife Jezebel, and the granddaughter of King Omri of Israel *(International Online Standard Encyclopedia)*. Her parents and grandfather were all Baalworshippers and arch enemies of God. They as well, possessed the same familiar spirit, and this spirit became stronger as it moved from generation to generation. By the time Athaliah began operating in it, she was so ruthless that once her husband Jehoram, and son Ahaziah died, she killed her own grandchildren to acquire the throne.

We have been taught through culture that we are to respect family, especially those who are older or hold a specific position with the family lineage. The challenge is, when you have a spirit like Athaliah within your family line, this spirit isn't looking to bond with the family. It is seeking an appointed time to strategically position itself so that it can rule, while either destroying or inheriting the fruit of that lineage. The challenge with the spirit of Athaliah is that it operates as a genocide, and will take out multiple family members consecutively. Moreover, if it can't operate to this extent, it will seek to continually wreak havoc in effort to steal the peace and unity within the family line.

Often the person within the family that has difficulty getting along with everyone else and/or who tends to constantly disrupt the family gatherings with ridiculous drama, is operating in this spirit. This spirit tends to latch onto the wounded within a family lineage, and because of his or her past hurts, feels justifiable in his or her actions when destroying the peace, unity and fruitful seed of the family. Athaliah had no problem killing her grandchildren to become ruler of Judah. She just didn't kill any family member, but sought to destroy the royal seed of her family line. This is significant as this spirit seeks to murder those that are heirs within the family lineage, but who are also significant heirs within the kingdom of God who have been strategically called to shift and establish God's kingdom. I state this because Athaliah's grandsons were the descendants of King David of which the Messiah, Jesus Christ was to be birth from *(Matthew 1:1-17)*. Those who uphold the standard of Jesus Christ and who God desires to use for His glory, often combat with this spirit. This spirit also seek to destroy the royal seed at a young age and if it is unsuccessful, it tends to seek the royal seed out in effort to harass and frustrate them such that it gains control over him or her or cause problems where the royal seeds misaligns with God thus relinquishing or exposing his or her position as the royal seed, or is in a position to be totally annihilated by this spirit.

There are instances that this spirit will have a person abort their own seed before he or she is even born, not realizing that he or she is killing off royalty. The Lord has often intervened during such cases by causing situations to occur where the royal seed isn't aborted but thus adopted or in Athaliah's grandson's case, hidden away till an appointed time where he or she can be revealed to reign and spiritually and naturally restore the monarchy of the family line.

2Chronicles 22:11-12:
> *(KJV)*
> *But Jehoshabeath, the daughter of the king, took Joash the son of Ahaziah, and stole him from among the king's sons that were slain, and put him and his nurse in a bedchamber. So Jehoshabeath, the daughter of king Jehoram, the wife of Jehoiada the priest, (for she was the sister of Ahaziah) hid him from Athaliah, so that she slew him not. And he was with them hid in the house of God six years: and Athaliah reigned over the land.*

As *Kingdom Heirs*, it is essential that we rise up and take our rightful place within our lineage if we really desire to see the blessings of the Lord and the restoration of being a monarchy within the lineage of Jesus restored in our family line. Though it isn't our desire to disrespect family members, it is important to expose and acknowledge these spirits within our family line and intercede against them so that they can be cast out of our lineage.

Often we are well aware of those within our family who are oppressed or possessed with this spirit, but we remain silent and inactive against it. If we do combat against it at family gatherings, we are often told to respect the person because of the position they hold within the family or for the sake of attempting to assert some form of peace. Yet truth is, there is only false peace when this spirit is around as its desire is to control the environment and maneuver into position where it rules over the dynamics of the family. God however, has designed this position for us as royal seeds. His word says,

1Peter 2:9-10:
> *(KJV)*
> *But ye are a chosen generation, a royal priesthood, an holy nation, a peculiar people; that ye should shew forth the praises of him who hath called you out of darkness into his marvellous light: Which in time past were not a people, but are now the people of God: which had not obtained mercy, but now have obtained mercy.*

Royal seeds are supposed to impact nations for the purposes of yielding glory to God. This glory comes through the lineage keeping the ways of the Lord, while releasing His will and judgment in the earth. We see this in Genesis when God informs Sarah and Abraham that they will have a child while also considering whether to share His plans to destroy the city of Sodom where Abraham's nephew Lot lived. God expressed that Abraham would become a large and strong family, whose generations would impact every family of the world.

Genesis 18:17-19

(KJV)
And the Lord said, Shall I hide from Abraham that thing which I do; Seeing that Abraham shall surely become a great and mighty nation, and all the nations of the earth shall be blessed in him? For I know him, that he will command his children and his household after him, and they shall keep the way of the Lord, to do justice and judgment; that the Lord may bring upon Abraham that which he hath spoken of him.

(Message)
Then God said, "Shall I keep back from Abraham what I'm about to do? Abraham is going to become a large and strong nation; all the nations of the world are going to find themselves blessed through him. Yes, I've settled on him as the one to train his children and future family to observe Gods way of life, live kindly and generously and fairly, so that God can complete in Abraham what he promised him."

(Amplified)
And the Lord said, shall I hide from Abraham [My friend and servant] what I am going to do, since Abraham shall surely become a great and

*mighty nation, and all the nations of the earth
shall be blessed through him and shall bless
themselves by him? For I have known (chosen,
acknowledged) him [as My own], so that he may
teach and command his children and the sons of
his house after him to keep the way of the Lord
and to do what is just and righteous, so that the
Lord may bring Abraham what He has promised
him.*

It is interesting that even though Abraham and Lot
were from the same family, Abraham was the one
that God chose to bless and release a great
generation that would divinely impact all of
mankind. All throughout the bible, God raised up
royal seeds within a lineage to impact nations.
These contenders experience great opposition
beyond that of the average saint and constantly
combated the spirit of death, because of the
significant call on their lives of impacting all
nations of the world. The spirit of Athaliah is one
of the key strongholds that attempt to sacrifice the
life of the royal seed to its idol god Baal such that a
nation is thus submitted to evil rather than to God.
If you read the history of Baal worship, you will see
that one of their practices is sacrifices, particularly
children. As *Kingdom Heirs* it is important that we
begin to assert Godly authority over our family
line. It is essential to align ourselves properly as
heirs such that this spirit is subjected to the power
of God, His will for the family line, and eventually
expelled from the lineage. This requires combating
this spirit in prayer, breaking the generational
curses that yield this spirit legal ground. It's also

important at times to confront this spirit naturally while exposing it for its true intent. Many family members won't understand your reason for exposing this spirit but it is this ignorance, lack of knowledge and submitting to this spirit that gives it the power necessary to remain rooted within the family line. This spirit relies on not being confronted and exposed and creating such havoc that people coward to it or leave it alone all together. We aren't after the person but we do seek to expose the spirit. Jesus never bowed to spirits. He sought to expose them and expel them. As *Kingdom Heirs*, we should be the same way. Some family members, especially those rooted in culture and tradition will be initially challenged by our actions, but in the long term of things, they will be grateful as the lineage shifts from the control of the enemy to the rule and reign of God.

ROYAL SEED TAKE YOUR PLACE

1Peter 2:9

> *(KJV)*
> *I declare that I have obtained God's mercy and I am of His chosen generation, a royal priesthood, a holy nation, a peculiar people. I show forth the praises of God who has called me out of darkness into His marvellous light.*

1. I rise up and take my rightful God given position as a *Kingdom Heir*....the divine royal seed of my family lineage.

2. I decree contentment with being chosen, and set apart as a royal priest, holy, and peculiar....unique in my divine purpose of who I am in the Lord.

3. I decree the blessings of the Lord is upon my family lineage and we keep His commandment of being fruitful, multiplying, subduing, and replenishing the earth spiritually and naturally (Genesis 1:28).

4. I decree my lineage is in covenant with Jesus Christ and as a *Kingdom Heir*, I claim divine rights to every seed, fruit, gifting, and blessing that my ancestors didn't operate in or possess. I call them out of captivity of the enemy and command them to realign with my family line in the name of Jesus.

5. I speak exposure, disruption and the excommunication of Jezebel, Ahab, Omri,

Ahazaiah, Athaliah and every other familiar
spirit and genocide of destruction, sabotage,
sin, and chaos that is lodged within my family
lineage. I decree your time has ended...you are
no longer welcomed and loosed from your
assignment eternally in the name of Jesus
(Matthew 16:19).

6. As a *Kingdom Heir*, I break every generational
curse associated with these entities and loose
the judgment of Jesus to eternally sever your
legalistic rights, ungodly trespasses, demonic
ties and evil effects (Galatians 3:13-14).

7. I decree my lineage shun the service,
dedications, and agreements with idol Gods
and false religions. We are life givers not life
takers. We do not offer sacrifices to idols, and
reject selling our birthright for the temporary
gains of the enemy and the world (Genesis
25:29-34).

8. My lineage has been adopted by my Lord and
Savior Jesus Christ and we belong to Jesus only.
It is in Jesus that we move, breathe and have
our very own being. It is in Him that we cry
Abba Father and assert our authority of
resurrection life and that more abundantly
(Galatians 4:6).

9. I contend that my lineage impact nations
worldwide, while lavishing immeasurable
glory upon the Lord.

10. As *Kingdom Heirs*, we proudly boast of the
miracles, signs and wonders of the Lord, and
His testimonies, works, character and nature is

honored and passed down from generation to generation (Deuteronomy 6:6-9).

PURSUING KINGDOM FULLNESS

God has been revealing to me that we have settled for a measure of the kingdom when Jesus overcame the enemy that we might have fullness in every aspect of our lives. The bulk of this book has been about us coming into our divine fullness; fullness of who we are in God, who He is in us, and fullness within our family line. As this book nears an end, it is essential to understand that a *Kingdom Heir* must establish authority over all that is under his or her reign and all that is available to his or her sphere of influence.

John 1:16

> *(Amplified)*
> *For out of His fullness (abundance) we have all received [all had a share and we were all supplied with] one grace after another and spiritual blessing upon spiritual blessing and even favor upon favor and gift [heaped] upon gift.*
>
> *(Message)*
> *We all live off his generous bounty, gift after gift after gift.*

This scripture declares that through Jesus we have the grace of fullness. We have the grace of receiving gift after gift after gift. That we no longer have to live in lack or limitation because Jesus works on the cross shifted us under grace to be restored in the life we were to have before the fall of man. This is an expectation we should not only wish we had but should be a standard we live by as we recognized it has already been attained for us.

Ephesians 3:20 asserts,
(KJV)
[20] Now unto him that is able to do exceeding abundantly above all that we ask or think, according to the power that worketh in us,

Power in the *Greek* is *Dunamis* and means:
1. act of power, miraculous power, ability
2. strength might, mighty work, miracles
3. natural capability, inherent power, capability of anything
4. not merely power capable of action but power in action

The power that works in us is not lacking. It is filled with potential and delivery beyond anything we can fathom or comprehend. As *Kingdom Heirs*, we must shift to an understanding that we are beyond limitation of this world and of the enemy. We must live from a knowledge that the only thing that can stop us is God and self.

Fullness in the Greek is *Pleroma* and means:
1. repletion or completion
2. what fills (as contents, supplement, copiousness, multitude), or

(objectively) what is filled (as container, performance, period)

3. that which is put in to fill up, piece that filled up fulfilling, full, fullness
4. abundance

The root word of *Fullness* is *Fill* which is pronounced *Pletoo* and means:

1. to make replete, (literally) to cram (a net), level up (a hollow), or

   (figuratively) to furnish (or imbue, diffuse, influence),
2. satisfy, execute (an office), finish (a period or task), verify (or coincide with a prediction), etc.
3. accomplish, (be) complete, end, expire, fill (up), fulfill, (be, make) full (come), fully preach, perfect, supply.
4. fulfill, fill, be full, complete, to make full, to fill up, to fill to the full
5. to cause to abound, to furnish or supply liberally abound, I am liberally supplied, to render full, i.e. to complete
6. to fill to the top so that nothing shall be wanting, to full measure, fill to the brim
7. to consummate to make complete in every particular, to render perfect
8. to carry through to the end, to accomplish, carry out, (some undertaking)
9. to carry into effect, bring to realization, realize, of matters of duty: to perform, execute

10. of sayings, promises, prophecies, to bring to pass, ratify, accomplish

11. to cause God's will (as made known in the law) to be obeyed as it should be, and God's promises (given through the prophets) to receive fulfillment

I shared all those definition in hopes of filling your spirit with the fullness of what it means to be a fulfilled *Kingdom Heir* of the Lord. It is a duty to pursue fulfillment. Not just fulfillment of destiny or doing God's will, yet fulfillment in living a life that radiates not only the sufferings of Christ but the blessings and fruit of Him suffering and resurrecting for us. When Jesus died, we died with Him and when He rose we rose with Him.

Romans 6:4
(KJV)
Therefore we are buried with him by baptism into death: that like as Christ was raised up from the dead by the glory of the Father, even so we also should walk in newness of life.

Romans 6:8
(KJV)
Now if we died with Christ, we believe that we will also live with him.

Newness in Romans 6:4 is *Kainotes* in the Greek and means:

1. renewal, newness

2. in the new state of life in which the Holy Spirit places us so as to produce a new state which is eternal life.

That means we rose into eternal life. Eternal life began when Jesus finished His three day death rest and rose up with all power in His hand. It began when we accepted Jesus as our savior and died and rose in covenant with Him. Therefore, the fullness and of the kingdom of God is now as we journey in our new life. We tend to receive the suffering and expect a little blessings here and there. But God's desires us to live in fullness. The more we embrace both sufferings and blessings as heritage, the greater miracles we will see in our lives and those around us. Let us shift to a position of expecting Him to move, expecting Him to fulfill, expecting Him to show forth on our behalf and on the behalf all that concerns us and our sphere of influence.

DECLARING KINGDOM FULLNESS

John 1:16

(Amplified)
*For out of His fullness (abundance) I have all
received [all had a share and I were all supplied
with] one grace after another and spiritual
blessing upon spiritual blessing and even favor
upon favor and gift [heaped] upon gift.*

(Message)
*I all live off his generous bounty, gift after gift
after gift.*

1. In the name of Jesus I cancel every seed and
   manifestation of lack, poverty, not enough, just
   enough, and emptiness, in my life and lineage
   (John 8:36, Romans 8:2, Galatians 5:1).

2. I expose death, murder, abortion, miscarriage,
   tragedy, with the blood and glory light of Jesus,
   and decree they are not the lot or substance of
   me or anything that concerns me. You are
   cursed, canceled and snuffed out to nothingness
   in the name of Jesus. I decree the life and
   resurrection power of Christ is solidified and
   eternally established in me and all that concerns
   us even now in the name of Jesus (Romans
   16:20, Colossians 2:14-15).

3. Grace and more grace, gift after gift,
   empowerment after empowerment, glory after
   glory, constant fulfillment and advancement is

raining on and ruling in me now in the name of Jesus (1 John 1:16, 2 Corinthians 3:16-18).

4. I am mounting up on wings of eagles, I am running and I am not weary.
   I am walking and not fainting (Isaiah 40:31).

5. For I expect fullness and nothing less (Psalms 24:1).

6. I pursue fullness and nothing less (Psalms 89:11).

7. I stand in fullness and nothing less (Colossians 1:19, Ephesians 4:13).

8. I reap fullness - its joy and everlasting pleasures and nothing less (Psalms 21:6).

9. Even now I bless God for being the author and finisher of my faith (Hebrews 12:2).

10. With unwavering relentless faith, I call forth the fullness of the cross and resurrection life of Jesus to be made manifested in me now in the name of Jesus (Hebrews 11:1).

11. Fullness of God's glory come now (Psalms 16:11).

12. Fullness of God's authority and power come now (Luke 10:19)!

13. Fullness of God's revelation, wisdom, understanding, counsel, and holy reverence, come now (Isaiah 11:2-3)!

14. Fullness of God's goodness and prosperity become my lot now (3 John 1:2)!

15. Fullness of the blood of Jesus and His healthiness, His wholesomeness...the fullness of the chastisement of His peace for my sake come upon me and all that concerns me now in the name of Jesus (Isaiah 53:5).

16. Fullness of God's love REIGN, and manifest within and through me.

17. Compassion, esteem and empowerment to bless others, receive fullness in me now (2 Corinthians 1:2-4).

18. Fullness of God's image, character, nature, personality, take form in me now (Genesis 1:27).

19. Fullness of holiness, righteousness, purity, invades me now.

20. Fullness to hate the things God hates and love the things God love and courage to face adversity for righteousness sake infuse my life now (Proverbs 6:16).

21. Fullness of God's promises, plans, will and destiny arise now (Isaiah 49:1-2).

22. Misalignment, be supernaturally corrected now. Disorder, receive order now. Hopelessness, receive hope now.

23. Every vision and kingly plan for me and my sphere of influence, receive the full victory and advantages to advance the kingdom now in the name of Jesus (Jeremiah 29:11).

24. Exceedingly and abundantly above all I can ask or think become my mantle of unwavering faith, now in the name of Jesus (Ephesians 3:20).

25. Constant refreshing and renewal, ravish me now in the name of Jesus (Proverbs 11:25)!

26. I proclaim and maintain that I am filled up in Jesus. I am overflowing in the plenty - fully complete and fulfilled in Jesus (Luke 6:38).

27. I give and more is given to me, in good measure, pressed down, shaken together and running over is given unto my bosom (Luke 6:38).

28. I eternally live and minister through kingdom overflow and consistent progression in the name of Jesus.

29. I decree that in every area of life and lineage, kingdom fullness has become my reality. I am a kingdom representation of God's fullness.

SHIFTERS & SHAKERS

As you already know, the name of my ministry is —*Kingdom Shifters Ministries.*‖ God has called us to preach the gospel but also to literally shift the world around us so that His presence, will, and kingdom can be established in the earth. We are hearing a lot about things shifting in the body of Christ at present so let's just explore what it means to —SHIFT!‖

Merriam Webster's Dictionary defines *Shift* as:

1. to exchange for or replace by another, change
2. to change the place, position, or direction of, to make a change in (place)
3. to change phonetically
   a. to change place or position
   b. to change direction
   c. to change gears
   d. to depress the shift key (as on a typewriter)
4. to assume responsibility
   a. to resort to expedients
5. to go through a change
   a. to change one's clothes
   b. to become changed phonetically

Genesis 1:1-4 states,

> (KJV)
> *In the beginning God created the heavens and the earth. And the earth was without form, and*

void; and darkness was on the face of the deep. And the Spirit of God moved upon the face of the waters. And God said, "Let there be light"; and there was light. And God saw the light, that it was good; and God divided the light from the darkness. And God called the light Day, and the darkness He called Night. And the evening and the morning were the first day.

<u>Moved</u> in the Hebrew is *Rachap* and means:

1. to brood, to be relaxed
2. to flutter, move, shake
3. to grow soft, relax, hover

Merriam Webster's Dictionary defines *Move* as:

1. to go or pass to another place or in a certain direction with a continuous motion
   a. to proceed toward a certain state or condition
   b. to become transferred during play
   c. to keep pace
   d. to start away from some point or place
   e. to depart
   f. to change one's residence or location
2. to carry on one's life or activities in a specified environment
3. to change position or posture, stir
4. to take action, act
5. to begin operating or functioning or working in a usual way

a. to show marked activity

b. to move a piece during one's turn

God's Spirit hovered, brooded, took action; proceeded towards a certain state or condition, etc. This means His spirit was in a position to fill or impregnate. God's Spirit was in route to reveal the spirit realm and make it tangible substance within the earth.

When God's presence began to move upon the face of the earth, it activated the unseen world of heaven, such that when He began to speak, materialization of His thoughts and will manifested to form earth. As *Kingdom Heirs*, we possess the literal presence of God, such that as when we preach the word, pray, encourage, perform miracles, walk in our giftings, or simply just walk into a place, the spirit realm should activate and materialize in our midst. There should be an immediate kingly change or future seed of impartation that follows our endeavors. As even if you can't transform a situation, there should be a seed sown that asserts God's authority so that someone else can come along to water and further grow what you planted. Let me say it another way. People should feel impacted and/or transformed and atmospheres should exemplify a release or impartation once encountering the God in us.

One day some friends and I were going into a store and a young man (teenager), approached us and asked if we wanted to purchase one of his rap CD's. The male teen was very polite and respectful, and assured us that though his CD wasn't Christian, it wasn't inappropriate. I asked the young man if we could pray for him, and though he said he believed in God, he immediately said, ―no.‖ He stated that he did not allow others to pray for him and we all laughed about it as I stated that I never seen anyone turn down prayer. I questioned the young man regarding the reason he didn't want prayer and even told him that if I prayed over him and his CD that he would be successful as God would profoundly bless his life. He stated that he was going to be successful anyway and was adamant, but respectful about not receiving prayer. We went on to subtly minister to the young man and I stated that I didn't want a CD but that I would impart a financial blessing into his musical endeavor. I however, expressed to the young man that my money was anointed and was just like prayer, that in taking my money, it was planting a seed into his life and his future. When I stated this, the young man said that he didn't want my money either and we politely imparted ways. After departing, we prayed for the young man as we drove away and claimed him and his gifting for the kingdom of God. He had encouraged us to view his videos on YouTube and when I did, I quickly learned that he was heavy into the rap image and had a strong desire for fame. A lot of his music is rooted in the worldly and idolatrous mindsets that rule that industry.

I was intrigued that the young teen understood the power of seed planting to the extent that he knew if he took my money it would be just like me praying for him and releasing a word into his life. He recognized that such an impartation had the power to change the dynamics of his life and he wasn't taking any chances on that happening. What he didn't consider is that just talking to us was an impartation, as one day he will remember that encounter, and it will be the catalyst for him recognizing the void that is missing from the destiny he so desperately seek.

Jesus impacted people in this way. Often when people left His presence, they were searching out things He spoke and did. Jesus was impacting and even more effectively, He was known for performing miracles, signs and wonders. He was a *Kingdom Shifter* such that regions were transformed by His very presence; for Jesus baffled and convicted people in towns where He wasn't well received; where because of their unbelief, He could only manifest a few miracles.

Mark 6:1-6

(KJV)

Then He went out from there and came to His own country, and His disciples followed Him. And when the Sabbath had come, He began to teach in the synagogue. And many hearing Him were astonished, saying, "Where did this Man get these things? And what wisdom is this

*which is given to Him, that such mighty works
are performed by His hands! Is this not the
carpenter, the Son of Mary, and brother of
James, Joses, Judas, and Simon? And are not
His sisters here with us?" So they were
offended at Him.*

*But Jesus said to them, "A prophet is not
without honor except in his own country, among
his own relatives, and in his own house." Now
He could do no mighty work there, except that
He laid His hands on a few sick people and
healed them. And He marveled because of their
unbelief. Then He went about the villages in a
circuit, teaching.*

Though the fullness of the kingdom of God was
available through Jesus, only a measure
manifested. Jesus left an impression that could be
watered or at least put the people in remembrance
that they were visited, yet rejected the Most High
God. Jesus shook the place up, and even though
many of the people weren't receiving of Him, they
knew a shift had occurred. Even if they didn't
have a name or enlightenment on what they had
experienced, they knew the glory that Jesus was
carrying was unique to what they knew about Him
and about God.

Further in this passage of scripture, we find that
when Jesus released the disciples, He told them
that if they aren't received, to shake the dust off
their shoes as testimony.

<u>**Verse 7-10**</u>

(KJV)

And He called the twelve to Himself, and began to send them out two by two, and gave them power over unclean spirits. He commanded them to take nothing for the journey except a staff – no bag, no bread, no copper in their money belts – but to wear sandals, and not to put on two tunics.

Also He said to them, "In whatever place you enter a house, stay there till you depart from that place. [11] And whoever will not receive you nor hear you, when you depart from there, shake off the dust under your feet as a testimony against them. Assuredly, I say to you, it will be more tolerable for Sodom and Gomorrah in the day of judgment than for that city!"

<u>*Shake* in the Greek is *Ektinasso* and means:</u>

1. to shake off so that something adhering shall fall

2. by this symbolic act, a person expresses extreme contempt for another, and refuses to have any further dealings with him

3. to shake off for (the cleansing of) one's self

What was falling off was judgment. The shaking of the shoe in this passage of scripture was a prophetic act that God's presence had come to visit a place. The shaking (falling) of the dust from the shoes was a prophetic cleansing and prophetic establishment that God's presence had visited and despite being revealed the truth, they had refused Him and thus would be judged for their actions once Jesus revisited the earth. For Jesus expressed further in this passage of scripture, that Sodom and Gomorrah would receive more grace than those cities that had received a shaking of dust for refusing the kingdom of God.

When one carries a true shifters anointing or release a word that something is shifting, what he are she is releasing is judgment, whether that be judgment against the enemy, judgment regarding the person or people, or the judgment for the release of God's kingdom and truth to manifest in a people or within that church, business, sphere or region. You are overriding the void and darkness and establishing the kingdom of God in its place.

Genesis 1:2-4
(KJV)
And the earth was without form, and void; and darkness was on the face of the deep. And the Spirit of God moved upon the face of the waters. And God said, "Let there be light"; and there was light. And God saw the light, that it was good; and God divided the light from the darkness. And God called the light Day, and the darkness He called Night. And the evening and the morning were the first day.

When something is void and dark, it is empty, vacant, obscure, ignorant; secrets that may not necessarily be good reside there. There is a possibility of death, destruction, wickedness, waste, ruin or it may lack a significant distinction. The void and the darkness itself isn't ALWAYS, (though sometimes it can be), a negative thing, but the lack of light posse a potential for harm to occur.

We see in Genesis, that as God's Spirit moved, He called forth light to the voided, darken earth. He judged the void and the darkness and commanded the light to come forth. The light brought forth illumination but nothing was actually created at that time. God's Spirit simply illuminated, materialized as light, to expose the true potential of what was available in the earth realm. God didn't remove darkness but, distinguished and established light from darkness by giving both a name and a function as —Day He called light & darkness He called Night.‖

When a matter receives illumination, knowledge materializes, revelation materializes; truth materializes. This means an impartation occurs. In this instance God didn't dispel darkness as He needed it for a specific function within the earth. Yet please know that there are times that darkness has to be totally displaced for light to come. However in this passage of scripture, there was an impartation of light, of truth and that in and of itself dispelled the void and the evils of darkness, while distinguishing that which is useful (the night) from that which has shifted and brought illumination (the day).

Romans 8:28

(KJV)

And we know that all things work together for good to those who love God, to those who are the called according to His purpose.

Shifters make things happen. They work and maneuver things in people, places, atmospheres so that God's purpose can manifest. *Shifters* can maneuver matters such that even the darkness can materialize kingdom good. Even if the *Shifter* is not received, is sent only to impart, or sent to totally annihilate the enemy, God's miracles, signs and wonders follow them.

It is time out for ministering voided message with no power following. It is time out for standing for causes and asserting judgments against people or sins, but lacking the power to actually manifesting change in people's lives and in regions. It is time out for just reading the Bible, hearing the word, but having minimal fruit of the kingdom being effectively activated in our lives and sphere of influence. As *Kingdom Heirs*, it's important to believe but also to seek God's will and words so that His shifting anointing can be active upon us, such that we illuminate, distinguish and establish His kingdom in people and in the earth. Forgive us Lord for just talking about You; Shift us to being about and actually revealing You and Your truth. *Kingdom Heirs* are *Kingdom Shifters*.

SHIFT! SHIFT! SHIFT!

1. Lord I am established in Your house and am certified as Your *Kingdom Heir*. Heir of God, Co-heir with Christ! Royal Priesthood to Your throne! SHIFT! (Romans 8:17).

2. As a *Kingdom Heir*, I declare I walk in the supernatural Dunamis power to not only to be about my Father God's business but to illuminate and produce His kingly business with signs following. I SHIFT! (Matthew 6:31).

3. I decree that I move, brood, impregnate and transform for the good all that I encounter in Jesus name. I DECLARE A SHIFT! (Genesis 1:1-4).

4. Even now I declare to my life and sphere, thy matchless kingdom come thy will be done in exceeding abundance, on earth as it is in heaven! SHIFT! (Matthew 6:10)

5. Thanks be to God whose fragrance I radiate as He causes all that I do to triumph! SHIFT! SHIFT! SHIFT! (2Corinthians 2:14).

6. I assert that Satan is under my feet! I crush His head and declare a kingdom suddenly! SHIFT! (Philippians 4:7)

7. For it is written that the kingdom of Heaven suffers violence and I the violent take it by force! I release a violent assault against all that binds and resists what God has for me! My life and region is empowered by God's authority! SHIFT! (Matthew 11:12)

8. You Oh Lord are the Only King and sovereign judge, who sits down one and promotes another! Promotion is my lot. I leap levels. I triumph over stagnation and a lack of progress. I declare forward motion only.
   Success only as I progress. I DECLARE A DESTINY SHIFT! (Psalms75:7)

9. Yes I'm a Kingdom overcomer! I overthrow all for greater are You in me than He that is in the world! I'm more than a conqueror through Christ Jesus who loves me dearly! With limitless authority I SHIFT! (Romans 8:37, 1John 4:4)

10. In Christ, old things have passed away, all things have become new! My newness is flourishing! It's illuminating! It's clarifying! It's defining and redefining! I SHIFT! (2Corinthians 5:17)

11. For I lack conformity to earthly standards of living and existing. I am transformed, freshened, and refurbished in my mind such that I respect and manifest God's truth! Truth of God noticeably manifest in me! I DECLARE I AM SHIFTING NOW! The SHIFT IS EVIDENT AND
    TANGEIBLE NOW! SHIFT! SHIFT(Romans 12:2, 1 Peter 2:9)

12. Great is my goodly kingdom heritage for the lines have fallen upon me in pleasant agreeable places! SHIFT! SHIFT! SHIFT (Psalms 16:6)

13. To everything there is a season; an appointed time, a specific occurrence under the sun! I

prosper in and out of season as even during winter seasons I am experiencing a kingly harvest! SHIFT! (Ecclesiastes 3:1)

14. For I am planted by the rivers of water, prosperous fruit is my eternal portion because my counsel is in not in wickedness but from heaven above! In health I prosper, In soul I prosper, In deed I prosper! SHIFT! (Psalms 1)

15. There are no limitations to the power of the Holy Spirit that is in me! I can do all things through Christ who invigorates, justifies, and regenerates me! SHIFT! (Philippians 4:13)

16. It is in my God that I live, I move, I breathe I have my very own being! There is no I, no me, no need to be without my Jesus. Abiding only in You produces a successful journey! I SHIFT! SHIFT! SHIFT!(Acts 17:28)

17. For with God, nothing is impossible. Therefore nothing is impossible through me. I declare the immeasurable awesomeness of God employs every endeavor of my kingly career, lineage, and all that concerns me! You God are the reason I exist! You are my purpose driven. You are my destiny! I align in Your timing and I SHIFT! SHIFT! SHIFT! (Luke 1:37)

References

Answers.com

Bible History Online, International Standard Bible Encyclopedia

Dictionary.com

Nolo's Plain English Law Dictionary

Cover Design and Layout:

Book Picture Cover is by James Parks and layout design by Reenita Keys

Connect with them via Facebook

Kingdom Shifters Books & Apparel
Available at Kingdomshifters.com

BOOKS FOR EVERYONE

Healing The Wounded Leader	Kingdom Shifters Decree That Thang
There Is An App For That	Kingdom Watchman Builder On the Wall
Embodiment Of A Kingdom Watchman Releasing The Vision	Dismantling Homosexuality Handbook Feasting In His Presence
Kingdom Heirs Decree That Thing	Let There Be Sight

Atmosphere Changers (Weaponry)

BOOKS FOR DANCERS

Dancers! Dancers! Decree That Thang

Spirits That Attack Dance Ministers & Ministries

TEE SHIRTS

Kingdom Shifters Tee Shirt	Let The Fruit Speak Tee Shirt
Releasing The Vision Tee Shirt Shirt	Kingdom Perspective Tee
Stand in Position Tee Shirt	No Defense Tee Shirt
My God Rules Like A Boss Tee Shirt	Destiny Blueprint Tee Shirt

CD'S

Decree That Thing CD

Kingdom Heirs Decree That Thing CD

www.ingramcontent.com/pod-product-compliance
Lightning Source LLC
LaVergne TN
LVHW051641080426
835511LV00016B/2434